THE
DAVIS
DISCIPLINE

Fifty Years of
Successful Investing on
Wall Street

John Rothchild

D1472334

John Wiley & Sons, Inc.

Published by John Wiley & Sons, Inc., New York.
Published simultaneously in Canada.

This publication is designed to provide accurate and authoritative information in
regard to the subject matter covered. It is sold with the understanding that the
publisher is not engaged in rendering professional services. If professional advice or
other expert assistance is required, the services of a competent professional person
should be sought.

ISBN 0-471-33178-3 (main volume)
ISBN 0-471-21637-2 (special edition)
ISBN 0-471-21634-8 (special edition)

Printed in the United States of America.

10 9 8 7 6 5 4 3

Foreword

B Y WEAVING THE FAMILY STORY IN AND AROUND the investing story, John Rothchild has written a lively and inspired account of this great stock-picking family. The narrative moves back and forth from Wall Street to the Davis household, so there's a constant interplay between the latest economic conditions and how the family responds to recessions, inflation, up markets and down. Also, the long-term perspective is a useful antidote to contemporary short-term thinking: Bull phases and bear phases have lasted many years.

On the personal front, we see how the elder Shelby Davis prepared his son (also Shelby Davis) to be frugal and to use stocks to build wealth. (Applying some of his father's techniques, his son ran a successful mutual fund.) On the economic front, the Davises adapted to the same challenges long-term investors will face in the future. No matter how big or small the portfolio, every household portfolio manager can benefit from reading this book.

I'd met the elder Shelby Davis several times during my career as manager of the Fidelity Magellan Fund. We talked at conferences, by telephone, and once or twice in my office, where we kicked around ideas about insurance and financial stocks.

I note with pleasure that the elder Davis followed many maxims I espouse in my own books, although in this case, I can't take any credit. He put these maxims into practice two decades before I did. His son and his grandsons have continued to apply some of the same stock-picking techniques I used at Magellan, and their overall view on investing sounds a lot like a Lynch sermon on the subject.

Rothchild's engaging and informative read may have a calming effect on the impatient household, as the Davises have stretched the time frame for long-term investing from one generation to three. They've been wedded to their portfolios for richer or for poorer, and eventually, the periods when stocks turned them poorer became trivial as compared to the overall enrichment. Moreover, their well-deployed capital has far outdistanced the typical paycheck. By owning insurance shares, the elder Davis did far better than most if not all the career executives who worked in the industry.

The popular and misguided notion that stocks are for the young, bonds for the old, is disproved here: for maximum compounding, stocks can be held indefinitely, while bonds outperform intermittently. Though investing early is preferable to investing late, the elder Davis also proved you don't have to start early to make a success of it. He was 38 when he began his insurance stock-picking adventure in 1947, and still he amassed the nine-digit fortune described in these pages.

I'm a vocal advocate of investing in things you know about, a tactic that is routinely ignored by doctors, engineers, and other professionals and nonprofessionals in the workforce. Witness the multitude that saw brown grass in their chosen fields and bought into the lush prognosis for dot.com speculations. The elder Davis, on the other hand, capitalized on information that came across his desk at a New York State agency that regulated insurance. Once he'd figured out how to decipher these corporate reports, he realized he'd stumbled onto a "mother lode," as Rothchild describes it. This was the late 1940s, when many insurance companies were sitting on hidden assets their stock prices didn't begin to reflect. Rather than idly marvel at these bargains, Davis took advantage of them. He quit his job, giving up a secure salary to go into business at his own insurance investment boutique. When he found he couldn't coax clients into buying shares, he took his own advice and bought them himself. Great investing requires an independent spirit, and the courage to acquire assets the crowd disdains. Disdain creates bargains.

For a brief stretch early in my tenure at Magellan, I sunk more than 15 percent of the fund's assets into insurance stocks. Six months later, when the fundamentals deteriorated, I changed my mind and scuttled most of these holdings. Thereafter, I'd occasionally find an insurer I liked (AFLAC, for instance), but I never specialized in any single type of enterprise or sector in the market. I found opportunity in small and large companies, domestic and foreign, fast growers and slower growers, prosperous companies and troubled companies that regained their former prosperity. In this eclectic approach, I differed from the Davises, but in one important area we had something in common. Some of my most rewarding investments came from slow-growth industries where expectations were low and profits lackluster. By looking for the most inspired competitors in uninspiring lines of work, I often found great growth enterprises (Toys "R" Us, La Quinta Motor Inns, and Taco Bell, for example) priced for mediocrity.

Similarly, in the insurance arena and later in the banking arena, Davis and his son bought shares in the best and brightest competitors for much less than they'd pay, say, for the best and the brightest in the hottest high-tech industries, which are always highly competitive and subject to sudden reversals of fortune.

You don't hear too many college kids say it's their dream to enter the property-casualty business, but while insurance may be unappealing to most, it has attracted a few outstanding operators like Hank Greenberg, who turned American

International Group into an on-going bonanza for shareholders since the 1970s. Davis' positions in AIG, and a dozen other companies with exceptional leaders, account for the bulk of his gains.

Davis easily could have afforded new tennis balls, but Rothchild reports he continued to play with ratty, old ones. This book is full of other examples of Davis's extreme frugality, and some readers may dismiss his tightwad tendencies as silly, or quirky, or perhaps annoying. But the wallet hugging impressed his children and his grandchildren that the surest way to build wealth is to spend less than you make and put the balance to work in stocks. With the U.S. savings rate at the lowest ebb in recent history, less spending and more saving would help the country and certainly benefit the savers.

Refusing to keep his wealth in the family by willing it to the next generation, Davis gave his son, also Shelby Davis, a gift that kept on giving: an understanding of the basics of compounding and a primer on how to pick stocks. This was a Wall Street version of teaching a hungry person to fish instead of giving him a filet. Davis decided to ship his filets to the universities, foundations, and think tanks he supported, while teaching his offspring to be a fisherman.

The younger Shelby eventually became a fund manager, and took over the New York Venture Fund in 1969, during the same period I was a rookie employee at Fidelity. We exchanged pleasantries, but never had lengthy exchanges. Shelby struck me as personable, down to earth, and devoted to his work. He didn't share his father's enthusiasm for insurance, but applied the Davis approach to other sectors.

Again, our styles differed: whereas I owned an ample supply of retail and restaurant chains that could grow their earnings at a 15 to 20 percent annual clip. Shelby avoided retail and prospected in the "foothills" with the steady but less spectacular 10 to 15 percent growers. Coming out of the bear markets of the early 1970s, we both avoided the beaten-down Nifty Fifty companies and looked for opportunities elsewhere. Sometimes, we ended up with the same names. We both loaded up on Fannie Mae, a once-troubled company that bought, sold, and packaged mortgages. We didn't buy troubled enterprises just because the stocks were cheap. We bought Fannie after we'd seen evidence it had put its troubles behind it.

We both found opportunity in the banking sector during the savings-and-loan crisis in the late 1980s. At one point, I'd taken stakes in scores of S&Ls—if a thrift was publicly traded, chances are it was in my portfolio. Shelby bought Citicorp when pundits debated its survival. Again, our familiarity with the workings of financial institutions gave us the confidence to buy when the news was bleakest. We knew our target companies were solvent, and the fundamentals were improving.

The elder Shelby Davis died in 1994, and the younger version retired from active fund management three years later. The third generation of Davises (Shelby's sons Chris and Andrew) is now in the process of proving itself with New York Venture Fund and other Davis funds. I'd be surprised if the same approach that worked for their grandfather and their father didn't work for them. Their expectations are neither overly optimistic nor pessimistic, which should keep them in the game.

We've all heard that people who are ignorant of history are doomed to repeat it. On Wall Street, history repeats itself routinely, as corrections and bear markets turn into bull markets sooner or later. Investors who are ignorant of this pattern aren't necessarily doomed, but they are likely to lose money trying to escape stocks at inopportune moments. Rothchild's book has drama, and offers wise counsel between the lines.

PETER S. LYNCH
Vice Chairman
Fidelity Management & Research Company

The Davis Family Timeline

1906–1909
Shelby Cullom Davis is born in Peoria in 1909. Earthquake and fires ravage San Francisco three years. Wall Street panic drops the Dow 32 percent, to a low of 53. Top-hatted financier J.P. Morgan saves U.S. banking system.

1928–1930
Davis graduates from Princeton; wife-to-be Kathryn Wasserman graduates from Wellesley. Both absorbed in international politics; disinterested in stock market, unaffected by the Crash of 1929; unaware of each other's existence.

1930–1931
Future investor (Shelby Davis) meets future wife Kathryn on French train. Both return to New York to pursue his-and-her graduate degrees at Columbia. At the onset of the Great Depression, studious couple isn't depressed.

1932
Studious couple marries in New York civil ceremony. Stock market bottoms, Dow at 41. Newlyweds ship out to Europe; Davis lands CBS radio job.

1933
Honeymoon over; Davis joins brother-in-law's investment firm—gets his first experience with stocks. Five-year stealth bull market enriches small minority who have cash and courage to buy. This surprise bonanza is often omitted from history of period, which features homeless hordes and unemployment lines.

1937
Davis quits brother-in-law's firm to pursue freelance writing. Bull market upended. As Dow drops from 194 to 98, Davis's son Shelby is born, creating disciple for as-yet-undeveloped Davis investment method.

1938

Davis's daughter Diana is born. Davis's book, *America Faces the Forties,* prepares to hit the bookstores. Satisfied reader Thomas E. Dewey (New York governor and presidential hopeful) hires Davis as economic adviser/speech writer.

1941–1942

Davis can't resist cheap price ($33,000), buys seat on New York Stock exchange. Dow backslides to 92, a price it first reached in 1906. America drawn into World War II.

1944

As a payback for Davis's consulting work, Governor Dewey names him deputy superintendent of insurance for state. Davis meets his mother lode: insurance companies. Wartime rally in stocks lifts Dow to 212.

1947

At age 38, Davis quits state government job to tend portfolio of insurance stocks, bought with $50,000 seed capital from Kathryn. Opens office near Wall Street. Nervous in peacetime, Dow slumps to 161 as investors worry that peacetime is bad for business. Experts advise: Buy bonds! Bonds respond perversely, as 34-year bear bond market begins.

1952

Davis is a millionaire on paper. It's taken 23 years, but Dow finally surpasses 1929 high mark of 381 for good.

1957

Davis's son Shelby graduates from Princeton and enters Wall Street workforce as stock analyst at Bank of New York. Stocks gallop ahead, on long march toward Dow 1000.

1962

In most rewarding trip of his lifetime, Davis flies to Japan, visits insurance companies, buys shares.

1963–1965
Third generation of Davis investors comes to life as Shelby's wife, Wendy, gives birth to Andrew and Chris Davis in Manhattan. Shelby exits Bank of New York to start small investment firm, along with two partners.

1965–1968
Mutual fund mania—not seen since 1920s. Dow flirts with 1000, a barrier that won't be broken for good for another 17 years. Pundits proclaim "new era" of perpetual prosperity brought on by promising tech sector. Stocks fall in first of three successive bear markets.

1969
Davis named ambassador to Switzerland; he and Kathryn pack up for Bern. Son Shelby and sidekick Jeremy Biggs take managers' jobs at New York Venture Fund. Second bear market in trilogy rattles investors; promising tech sector gets clobbered.

1970
New York Venture Fund is top one-year performer, lauded in *Business Week;* soon to become bottom performer.

1973–1974
Third bear market in trilogy, worst decline since 1929 to 1932. Takes Dow on 45 percent plunge from 1051 to 577. Prestigious Nifty Fifty companies take deeper plunge—down 70 to 90 percent. Original New York Venture Fund shareholders left with zero profit after five years.

1975
Ambassador Davis returns from Switzerland, is reunited with $20 million portfolio worth $50 million three years earlier. Shelby divorces Wendy, soon marries Gale Lansing. Adopts new stock-pricing methods resulting in string of winning years for New York Venture Fund.

1981
Wild inflation of 1970s finally corralled. Interest rates begin 20-year fall. Stocks begin 20-year rise, but only optimistic pariahs predict it.

1983
With Shelby as solo manager, New York Venture Fund beats S&P 500 for seventh straight year.

1987
Stocks crash. Global panic. Davis goes on buying spree.

1988

Davis makes *Forbes* list of 400 richest Americans; he has a $427 million portfolio. Shelby makes *Forbes* honor roll for reliable mutual fund excellence.

1990

Chris takes job in grandfather's office in New York.

1991

Chris installed as manager of Davis Financial Fund. Dow hits 3000.

1993

Andrew takes charge of Davis Convertible and Real Estate Funds (created with him in mind). Moves to Santa Fe.

1994

Davis dies, leaving nearly $900 million in trust for conservative causes. Shelby and Chris sell Davis's holdings and invest the proceeds in the New York Venture Fund and other Davis funds. Davis assets and brain power are finally united in same accounts.

1995

Chris named comanager of the New York Venture Fund. Andrew happy with a less dramatic role. Dow hits 5000.

1997

Shelby turns 60, the New York Venture Fund turns 28. Chris named sole manager of the Fund with Shelby consulting from sidelines. Shelby donates $45 million of his own fortune to the United World College scholarship program, a signal to his children that they won't inherit his bundle, just as he didn't inherit Davis's fortune.

1998–2000

Andrew, Chris, and Chris's new partner, Ken Feinberg, cope with a tired bull market.

Contents

xiii

INTRODUCTION

HIS PROJECT BEGAN AS A BOOK ABOUT SHELBY Davis, the fund manager. Without much fanfare, Shelby's New York Venture Fund had given investors a great ride: An investment of $10,000 had turned into $379,000 during his 28-year stewardship. In 22 of those years, he beat the market. This record put him in a league with Peter Lynch at Fidelity with the Magellan Fund. I was curious. How did he do it?

We met for dinner at a seafood place in Palm Beach, Florida. We were surrounded by gray hair and blue blazers. Shelby wore the latter. He had a slight build and a boyish face. He was amusing and modest. He steered the chitchat away from himself and toward the latest quarterly report from Hewlett-Packard. He admired the way Fannie Mae grew its earnings in good markets and bad. He made the merger between Wells Fargo and Norwest banks sound as exciting as a French tryst.

We had a follow-up discussion on the 97th floor of the World Trade Center in New York, where Shelby kept an office. There, at the conference table, he filled in details about his excellent—though not particularly celebrated—career. According to him, the major influence on his savvy stockpicking was another Shelby Davis—his father. (The older Davis had confused the issue by pulling a George Bush and naming a son after himself without a "junior" attached. To keep them straight in the pages that follow, I'm calling the father "Davis" and the son "Shelby" throughout.) "The old man was a better investor than I was," Shelby said, pitching his father as an interesting book subject in itself. "He turned $50,000 into $900 million. Insurance stocks, mostly."

Nine hundred million dollars was an attention grabber. Shelby elaborated. Davis was a former freelance writer, GOP campaign adviser, and Dilbert in the New York State Insurance Department. In 1947, at age 38, with no MBA and no formal economics training, he quit his job to become a full-time prospector in the insurance sector. Friends and relatives were skeptical. This was before the midlife crisis was invented. Otherwise, they would have suspected Davis was having one.

Over the next four and a half decades, Davis skillfully chauffeured his portfolio into one of the great Wall Street fortunes. Basically, he stuck with insurance stocks through booms, busts, bebop, beatniks, and the Beatles. When U.S. insurers got too pricey, he bought Japanese insurance stocks. In the 1960s, his Japanese holdings took off like pigeons near a firecracker. By the time he died, in 1994, he'd multiplied his original stake 18,000 times.

This wasn't a rags-to-riches yarn; it was more like Saks-to-riches. The source of Davis's original stake was his wife, Kathryn Wasserman, daughter of a Philadelphia carpet mogul. Most Americans in 1947 could only dream of spending $50,000 on a stock portfolio. Still, the result was an inspirational and hopeful tale: This former freelance writer started investing in middle age and became a near billionaire in his lifetime. Yet, outside insurance circles, the first Shelby Davis was almost as obscure as the second.

"My father made the *Forbes* list of wealthiest Americans in 1988," Shelby said. "His 15 seconds of fame." The *Forbes* reference reminded me of the lack of so-called "passive investors" on that magazine's wealth parade. Among the numerous Silicon Valley whizzes, corporate raiders, real estate developers, inventors, retailers, manufacturers, media czars, oil barons, bankers, and others who routinely appeared on the list, I could think of only one other person who got there by picking stocks in other people's companies: Warren Buffett.

I asked Shelby if his father and Buffett had ever met. "A few times," he said. "They were acquaintances. They had a lot in common." Shelby elaborated. Both had "grown" their money at an impressive 23 to 24 percent annual rate for decades. Both made their biggest profits from insurance stocks, and Buffett owned two insurance companies outright. Was it mere coincidence that these two shareholding prospectors found buried treasure in the industry that was shunned by Wall Street sophisticates as "stodgy," "boring," and "unrewarding"? The insurance angle was intriguing. Should we all be buying insurance stocks?

Both were notorious tightwads who lived far beneath their means. Davis wore shoes with holes and sweaters that were moth-eaten, and he played endless sets of tennis with the same used balls. Buffett wore frumpy suits and ferociously hoarded trivial sums. According to Buffett's biographer, Roger Lowenstein, Buffett was already a multimillionaire when a traveling companion told him she needed to make a quick call at an airport pay phone. (A dime was the going rate at the time.) Buffett fished a quarter from his pocket, but rather than hand the excessive coin to his anxious friend, he walked a long corridor to find a newspaper stand that made change.

As their fortunes moved into seven, eight, and nine figures, both men continued to live in the modest houses they had bought in the 1940s and 1950s, respectively: Davis in Tarrytown, New York; Buffett in Omaha, Nebraska. When Buffett's wife bought $15,000 worth of furniture for their modest abode, it "just about killed Warren," a family friend was quoted in Lowenstein's biography, *Buffett: The Making of a Capitalist*. "Do you realize," Buffett said, "how much that is if you compound it over 20 years?" Davis gave the identical speech to his grandson when he refused to buy the boy a $1 hot dog.

Once he'd broken through the billionaire barrier, the folksy Buffett suffered a spending lapse and bought a corporate jet. He called it the Indefensible. Davis never bought so much as a Piper Cub.

The Buffett/Davis comparison can be carried too far. Buffett was a billionaire twenty times over; he often headed the *Forbes* roster. Davis's name, although listed many times, was inconspicuous in the middle of the list. Buffett's accomplishments were well lauded. Davis's were all but unknown. I mulled Shelby's suggestion to write only about his father—something along the lines of "Best Investor You Never Heard Of," or "Secrets from the World's Second Greatest Stock Picker."

Davis wasn't around to provide details. He died in 1994, leaving a fortune in paper assets but little in the way of a paper trail. He'd kept no journals or diaries, and he never bothered to preserve back copies of his weekly insurance letter. Innermost thoughts, such as "Buy 100 shares Chubb," he scribbled on old envelopes or ticket stubs, to avoid wasting money on note pads. These scribbles, too, were lost to the trash bin.

Cronies and sidekicks from the early stages of Davis's investing were fading fast. His wife, Kathryn (Shelby's mother and the source of the original $50,000), agreed to reminisce, but the spry nonagenarian drew a blank on her husband's financial maneuvers. Husbands from her generation believed in the separation of commerce and wives.

The most informative source on Davis was his namesake, the fund manager I was interested in writing about in the first place. Born in 1937, Shelby had grown up watching his father analyze companies, tagged along to visit CEOs, learned how money went forth and multiplied, as determined by the Rule of 72. That simple calculation put an exciting spin on the familiar adage penned by the overfed founding father, Ben Franklin. Not only was a penny saved a penny earned—a penny compounded 25 times was $671,000!

People who buy lottery tickets know that the chance of winning a million is less than the chance that O.J. was innocent based on the DNA evidence. If a young person with a $10-a-week lottery habit could forgo the fantasy and invest the weekly $10 in a typical mutual fund that returns an annual 10 percent (modest by Davis's standards), becoming a millionaire in 30 years will be guaranteed. To his son, Davis passed along his infectious passion for owning shares in carefully chosen companies (he called them "compounding machines"), his conviction that owning the best compounding machines would lead to unimagined rewards, his distrust of unnecessary spending (why waste money that could be invested?), and his workaholic tendencies. Shelby readily acknowledged that his success as a fund manager resulted from his childhood training. Not only had Davis devised a winning portfolio that paid off over a half-century of stock market gyrations, the frugal workaholic prepared his son to continue the tradition with the same obsessive verve.

Into early adulthood, Shelby was his father's clone. He prepped at Lawrenceville (Davis's boarding school), graduated from Princeton (Davis's alma mater), worked on the college paper (Davis did, too), and married into a wealthy family (same as Davis). Like his father, Shelby studied history and learned the rudiments of accounting, balance sheet diving, and Security Analysis 101 on the side. Like his father, he valued the intangibles of corporate leadership more than tangibles on spreadsheets. He never let a statistical forest block his view of the trees.

Like his father, he rejected the MBA route. By word and by deed, Davis had persuaded Shelby that Wall Street's most popular degree produced a stupefying conformity, which Davis had profitably avoided. Davis zigged when others zagged. He bought stocks when most experts flogged bonds, and he pocketed insurance shares when others avoided them. Shelby showed similar independence. Like his father, he quit secure employment (his at a bank) to launch his stockpicking career.

By keeping his wallet zipped, Davis maximized the capital he then invested for maximum return. He disapproved of excessive corporate spending as much as he disapproved of excessive household spending, and he tended to buy companies whose managers were as frugal with their investors' dollars as he was with family dollars.

His favorite CEOs were flinty kindred spirits—cost-conscious workaholics like AIG's Maurice "Hank" Greenberg. He limited his portfolio to AIG and other insurance stocks because they generally sold at a sizable discount to the typical noninsurance issue, and a huge discount to the latest investment fad—usually, something high-tech that soon became high-wreck. His refusal to overpay for things gave him the discipline to buy frugal enterprises at giveaway prices. Thus, his philosophy for daily life, corporate life, and Wall Street life put him in the growth-at-a-reasonable-price camp, as opposed to the dangerously fashionable growth-at-any-price camp.

Finally, so the compounding and wealth building didn't end with his demise, he taught his children obsessive frugality. The entire family pinched pennies as the millions piled up, although until they reached their twenties, the children were generally unaware the millions existed. Shelby and Diana were raised on farmer's chores: stack wood, rake leaves, gather eggs from chicken coops, shovel snow. They were taught never to order lobster or fresh orange juice in a restaurant. Davis acceded to their request for a backyard swimming pool on one condition: The family had to dig the hole.

His goal was to create self-reliant offspring who didn't depend on family largesse, so his accumulated pile could be spared for the worthiest causes. In keeping with the compounding theme, Davis planned to leave his wealth to organizations that promoted free enterprise and opposed political threats to capitalist momentum. Thus, his money would help ensure that the U.S. system continued to allow others to successfully deploy their capital, without overtaxing and overregulating their efforts. With investor-friendly leadership, the nation at large could continue to maximize prosperity.

Through the first two decades of our saga, Davis triumphed with his all-insurance portfolio. By the 1950s, Shelby had reached adulthood. He worked for The Bank of New York for eight years, then left to start an investment boutique with two friends. Soon, their small company took control of the fledgling New York Venture Fund. In his rookie year as manager, Shelby rode hot tech stocks to the top of the performance charts. In his second year, the bear market of 1969 to 1970, he rode those same stocks to the bottom of the performance charts. Like a writer in search of his voice, Shelby tinkered with his portfolio, searching for a strategy that suited him.

After a subsequent bear market, in 1973 to 1974, the New York Venture Fund was on the upswing. By trial and error, he cobbled his own style, based on but not mimicking his father's approach. Instead of filling the Funds with insurance stocks

8

exclusively, Shelby branched out and invested in banks, brokerage houses, and other companies that shared key attributes with his father's favorite insurers. He bought "growth companies at a bargain price" and outdistanced all but a handful of rival mutual funds.

Davis returned to the United States in 1975, after serving as ambassador to Switzerland. He'd suffered big losses in the twin bear markets mentioned above, and his net worth had dropped from $50 million to $20 million. But then his insurers rebounded and, by the mid-1980s, his portfolio, too, was compounding at a rapid rate. Soon, the $30 million short-term loss looked trivial. He gained $750 million in the next 15 years.

So far, we've identified the Davis era, when Davis applied his principles alone, and the Shelby era, when the son and his father invested simultaneously but not in concert. Next came the Chris and Andrew era. Their grandfather was in decline, Shelby was continuing the New York Venture Fund tenure, and his two sons managed their own mutual funds on the Davis strategy.

Raised in the 1960s and 1970s, Chris and Andrew learned about the magic of compounding and the Rule of 72, the family's complement to the Golden Rule. As a teenager, Chris worked part-time in his grandfather's office on weekends. Summers, he signed on as cook and chauffeur at the Davis house in Maine. He got along well with both sides of the Davis/Shelby divide.

Before he got to Wall Street, Chris passed through a "Viva Fidel" phase, when he denounced the "running dogs of capitalism"; a Dr. Doolittle phase, when he thought about becoming a veterinarian; and a Father Flanagan phase, when he flirted with the priesthood. From there, he veered into a Davis orbit, enrolling in a training program at a Boston bank, then taking a job at a small New York investment house. In 1989, his grandfather hired him as his apprentice. Chris eagerly accepted.

Andrew, meanwhile, took a less eccentric route into the Davis domain. He majored in economics and business at Colby College in Maine, then worked for Shawmut Bank in Boston and PaineWebber in New York, before taking control of two funds (real estate and convertible bonds) that Shelby had launched with Andrew in mind.

The patriarch was ailing. In 1990, at age 81, Davis suffered a stroke. Convinced that Chris had made the most of his apprenticeship, Shelby hired Chris away from his grandfather to manage Davis Financial, another new fund intended to give the next generation a chance to prove itself.

Shelby held his father's hand as Davis died in 1994. Davis's ashes were buried in Maine and his assets were scattered among the Davis funds, so the spoils from two great investors were united at last. The next generation was now in charge of them.

This book is about investing in the long term, where the long term isn't 15 minutes, or until the next quarterly report, or even until the next economic cycle. Buying and holding is all the rage these days, and the Davises provide a 50-year case study not only in how to tend a portfolio but how to raise privileged children who break the trustafarian mold, work hard, earn their own keep, and allow the family fortune to continue to compound. Theirs is true long-term investing: not five years, or ten years, but perpetual. Their financial escapades cover the period from the late 1940s, when most Americans were afraid to own stocks, through the 1990s, when most Americans were afraid *not* to own stocks. Along the way, they invested through two lengthy bull markets, 25 corrections, two savage bear markets, one crash, seven mild bear markets, and nine recessions; three major wars; one presidential assassination, one resignation, and one impeachment; 34 years of rising interest rates and 18 years of falling interest rates; a lengthy struggle with inflation; stretches when bonds gained while stocks lost, or stocks gained while bonds lost, or gold gained while both bonds and stocks lost; and even a stretch when a savings account was more rewarding than the Dow in all its glory. As we see how the Davises negotiated these twists and turns, we learn about how stocks behave through good times and bad.

Looking through the Davis family tree, Mr. Market's twentieth-century history can be reduced to three periods of great gain and two periods of great loss, with interludes of drift and gradual recovery in between. The gains were made between 1910 and 1929, 1949 and 1969, and 1982 to the present. In each of these roughly 20-year uplifts, stocks were helped along by a fat economy, gee-whiz technology, rising corporate profits, and soaring valuations. Consumers had disposable cash and an inclination to spend it.

The two periods of great loss occurred from 1929 to 1932 and from 1970 to 1974. Most of the stock market wealth created between 1921 and 1929, and again between 1949 and 1969, disappeared in these pecuniary debacles. If you owned the hottest stocks in the hottest industries, your losses were maximized. Moreover, because the public was slow to buy on the way up, the mass of small investors came out of the round trip poorer for the experience. Investing via mutual funds was regarded as safer than buying naked stocks, but the average fund declined as much as, or more than, the average stock.

During the rebuilding phases, stocks drifted, rallied, and suffered demoralizing swoons. From the 1932 bottom, the rebuilding took more than 20 years; from the 1974 bottom, nearly eight years. In each restorative yin-yang, the public fell out of love with equities.

Throughout the market saga and the family saga, Davis stock-picking techniques have produced many happy returns, and readers may profit from applying them.

CHAPTER 1

SHELBY CULLOM DAVIS

HELBY Cullom Davis was born in 1909, in a nice neighborhood in the town that inspired the famous question: Will it play in Peoria? On the family tree, a passenger on the *Mayflower* dangled from his mother's branch and an original inhabitant of Jamestown looked down from his father's. His namesake and great-uncle, Shelby Cullom, was a one-term governor of Illinois, a four-term fixture in the U.S. House of Representatives, and a six-term fixture in the U.S. Senate.

For all the kickbacks, sweetheart deals, and other get-rich-quick schemes foisted on the electorate by the elected, it's a surprise that U.S. politics didn't create notable or lasting fortunes the way Third World politics did in the twentieth century. Journalists in every U.S. town, city, and county found plenty of corruption to write about, but corruption was somewhat democratic—otherwise, for all the money floating around, why didn't America develop a ruling class of millionaire mugwumps? Powerful senators with *Mayflower* pedigrees might have dined out on their lineage, but the lineage per se didn't pay the bills.

Davis's great-uncle Shelby Cullom wasn't in politics for the money. In fact, he devoted his political career to fighting the "moneyed magnates" who ran the railroads. He opposed Harriman, Vanderbilt, and other railroad tycoons as surely as he opposed polygamy. One man, one wife was a campaign issue in the nineteenth-century American farm belt, along with fair prices for farm freight.

Once the magnates had bought or driven off their competitors on key rail routes, they charged gougers' rates to ship cattle, wheat, corn, and other comestibles. Envisioning the same hordes of dollar signs, tycoons in other industries, from baking to matchbook making, conspired to monopolize. Faced with an epidemic of monopolizing, consumers cried "Foul!" and Washington responded. Congress passed and the courts upheld new laws to restore free enterprise through stricter regulation. Davis's great-uncle was part of this welcome, albeit ironic, solution. He pushed for the Interstate Commerce Commission, which was created in 1887 to thwart the railroad cabal. In 1912, at age 82, Senator Cullom was elected to a sixth and final term. He died in office. Davis, then age five, marched in the funeral procession.

In Cullom's lifetime, America's fastest-growing industry was railroads. Its managers, Davis later wrote, were "like generals of a vast Army." The iron-and-cinder superhighway—an ancient precursor to the Internet superhighway—excited imaginations and attracted more investors than any construction job in history. From the mid-1800s and beyond, the public paid for the laying of track coast-to-coast and exchanged cash for a never-ending supply of stocks and bonds. With the stock market in disfavor, railroad companies preferred to finance their expansion with bonds. In theory, these corporate IOUs were safer than stocks because issuers were obligated to refund bondholders' money, plus interest, while the issuers of stock had no obligation to stockholders. In fact, however, the "safer" alternative proved hazardous to at least two generations of railroad investors. Having gone the bond route, railroads were saddled with huge interest payments they often failed to make. During recessions and other crises, they solved their cash flow problems by defaulting on their paper and by drifting in and out of bankruptcy.

Investors in the "vast Army" learned an expensive lesson: There is no guarantee that a fast-growing industry with great future promise will reward its financial backers along the way. Railroads had been lauded as the nation's most reliable blue-chip companies, yet the payoff was unreliable at best. Stockholders saw their "conservative" rail holdings marked down in frequent panics and bear markets; bondholders were lucky to escape with their money back.

Foreign investors were the biggest losers in U.S. rail projects. The British, in particular, couldn't resist bankrolling the emerging U.S. market in the mid-1800s, just as Americans couldn't resist bankrolling emerging Asian markets in the late 1900s. Much British capital was lost in what turned out to be a gigantic, albeit unintended, charitable contribution to U.S. track laying and road building. Heed it well, ye global capitalists! Fast growth in the latest emerging phenom doesn't necessarily mean fat profits for foreign enthusiasts. The U.S. railroads proved that.

Davis was too young to grasp railroad finance, and his immediate family (father George, mother Julia Cullom) had nothing to do with stocks or bonds. They lived comfortably in Peoria, thanks to the income stream that came from a corner storefront owned by the family. This income stream subdued George Davis's pecuniary ambitions.

After he studied architecture at Princeton, George Davis had a brief and successful entrepreneurial debut. During the Alaskan Gold Rush, in 1898, he hustled out to the Pacific Northwest but arrived too late in the season to find and stake out a promising claim. Hearing that many earlier arrivals had neglected to bring winter feed for their horses, he chartered a barge in Seattle, filled it with hay, and shipped the load to Alaska. The hay was quickly sold out, at sellers' market prices. Prospecting in a mundane substance, George Davis outperformed all but a tiny percentage of the gold diggers. On a larger scale, Levi Strauss did the same thing with pants.

Once he'd returned to Peoria to marry into the Cullom clan, George Davis practiced architecture intermittently, if at all. He dressed like a Wall Street banker, insisted people call him "judge" (a nickname from college) and passed the time writing letters to the editor and picking up the monthly stipend from the storefront. He referred to this errand as "attending to my affairs."

Throughout Davis's childhood, the proceeds from the storefront rental provided a comfortable living: a local country club membership plus a prep-school-and-Princeton education for him and his brother, and enough cash left over to reward the two boys annually with $1,000 for not smoking. Their father, who suffered from lung disease and smoked, didn't want the mistake repeated.

Growing up with a ne'er-do-well father prepared the world's second greatest stock picker for successful investing, in a backhanded sort of way. From an early age, Davis was determined to work hard and avoid family welfare and all its degrading side effects. He held a variety of summer and afternoon jobs in Peoria. Family lore has him standing on a street corner, hawking a stack of newspapers that announced the end of World War I. This was standard schoolboy stuff, not nearly as imaginative as the enrichment scheme hatched by the world's greatest stock picker, Warren Buffett. According to his biographer, young Buffett paid his pals to dive for golf balls in the water hazards at the local links in Omaha, then sold the balls back to the pro shop.

Davis was long gone from Peoria by the time the Great Depression retarded the income stream and forced his family to economize. His father, the "judge," discovered frugality. "Use it up, wear it out, make do or do without," was George Davis's motto and mission. He took the mission so seriously that once—on a trip East to visit his son—he stopped at a train station, found the telegraph office, and wired a reminder back to his wife: "When you leave the house, don't forget to unplug the electric clock!"

Scholastically, Davis excelled at Lawrenceville and at Princeton. He was the managing editor of the campus newspaper at each school. At Lawrenceville, he was voted most likely to succeed. At Princeton, he joined a second-tier social club—Charter—then threatened to quit when Charter blackballed his Jewish roommate, Trivers. He stuck with Charter (at Trivers's behest) but preferred to socialize with a less starchy crowd. He shared the Bohemian disdain for conspicuous consumption: raccoon coats, silver flasks, gold watches, and so on. His father's frugality had rubbed off and later would pay off. His habit of living beneath his means freed his capital to make the most of itself.

Davis the student showed no interest in economics or finance. He majored in history and read widely on the Russian revolution. The first U.S. financial best-seller, *Common Stocks as Long-Term Investments,* appeared in the bookstores in 1924, when Davis was in prep school. The author, Edgar Lawrence Smith, argued that stocks were reliable and worth owning, even by widows and orphans. This contradicted conventional wisdom that pegged stocks as Wall Street's answer to a wager on a horse. Using words that will sound familiar today, Smith observed that Americans lived in a "New Era" of fantastic pecuniary promise.

In these "modern, enlightened times," Smith wrote of the mid-1920s, investors and consumers stood to benefit from the "emerging science of corporation management" that gave U.S. firms a lucrative advantage in the global marketplace.

At its 1921 low, the Dow traded at 63, a price it had fetched back in 1888. As prices rose toward the 1929 top of 381, so did the public's acceptance of Smith's enthusiasm. People who'd shunned the market a decade earlier eagerly embraced it late in the rise. Pioneer U.S. mutual funds—Massachusetts Investors' Trust, and State Street Investing Company—opened for business in Boston. The typical investor sought dividends, not earnings, and blue-chip railroad issues continued to attract a conservative faction looking for a safe return. At this point, the rails were called "America's 20 percent industry," because they bought 20 percent of all the iron, steel, coal, timber, and fuel oil produced and sold inside the country. The bullish line was that railroads had outgrown their untrustworthy adolescence and were now too well-established to fail. The railroad index had more than doubled over the decade.

Whether Davis read Smith's book is anybody's guess, but it made such a splash, he couldn't have avoided hearing about it, nor could he have avoided the gleeful newspaper accounts of quick fortunes made by the "margin millionaires" who borrowed their way onto Easy Street.

Though he was a quarter-century away from investing in earnest, Davis met his future bankroll on a French train. Textiles, not the storefront in Peoria, produced his seed capital, siloed in the trust funds of the woman sitting across the aisle. Kathryn Wasserman sized up her husband-to-be: ski-slope tan, tweedy British jacket, leather arm patches for sophistication— the uniform of the Ivy Leaguer. She noticed that his body language (shy eyes, slumped shoulders) didn't fit his preppy clothes. She sensed his discomfort with women. Figuring he'd never speak first, she broke the ice: "Is Geneva the next stop?"

They discovered they were both getting off at Geneva. They'd enrolled at the same Swiss summer school, sponsored by the Rockefellers, where bright students from around the world coagulated. The Rockefellers hoped a few of these high IQs would run their countries' governments someday, remember the fun they had together, and refuse to fight wars with one another. The goal was optimistic, and already the school had produced one promising alliance in transit: Davis and Wasserman.

Davis had a *Mayflower* pedigree; Wasserman, an Ellis Island pedigree. But they found they had a lot in common. Both attended status colleges (Princeton, Wellesley). Both studied Russian history. Both traveled in and around Russia before heading for Switzerland. Davis visited Leningrad and Moscow on an academic junket; Wasserman rode a horse through the wilds of the Caucasus. She slept in tents, shared campsites with gypsies, bartered with tribal chieftains, and rebuffed numerous lechers.

CHAPTER 2

A LAST HURRAH
FOR BONDS

After the great market decline of 1929 to 1932, all common stocks were widely regarded as speculative by nature. A leading authority stated flatly that only bonds could be bought for investment.
Benjamin Graham, *The Intelligent Investor*

HELBY WAS BORN IN 1937; HIS SISTER, DIANA, IN 1938. Soon after Diana's birth, Davis was hired by Governor Dewey, and the family exited Philadelphia and moved to Scarborough-on-Hudson, New York, where they rented the guest quarters on a local estate. Kathryn hired a baby nurse and a cook—household help was cheap in the area. She volunteered part-time for the League of Women Voters. Davis worked in Albany, in the governor's office, and came home on weekends. After Dewey lost the presidential nomination at the 1940 GOP convention, Davis returned to freelancing. He was named financial editor of *Events* magazine, an offshoot of the widely read *Current History*. He wrote a series of lengthy articles on key U.S. industries (shipping, steel, and so on) for the *Atlantic Monthly*, and knocked off another book: *Your Job in Defense.*

In 1941, Davis invested in Wall Street in a curious, backhanded way. Kathryn had saved $30,000—her father had provided all his children the same amount so each of them could buy a house. Davis and Kathryn had continued to rent because Davis thought houses were too expensive to maintain. Then, in 1941, the man who had refused to spend family money on a house bought a seat on the New York Stock Exchange. He had no use for the seat, purchased from one Nathaniel S. Seeley. At this point, reviving his short-lived career in the investment business hadn't occurred to him. He bought it because he couldn't resist the $33,000 price tag. An identical seat had fetched $625,000 in 1929. To Davis, it was like finding a valuable antique at a garage sale.

A year after his purchase, identical seats were selling for $17,000, so Davis didn't catch the absolute bottom of the stock exchange membership trade. Still, he'd bought very low. The seat market rallied to $97,000 in 1946, then stalled in the early 1950s but never fell below $33,000. By the time Davis died in 1994, his seat was worth $830,000 (May 1994). Buying stingy became a Davis hallmark.

Families nationwide subsisted on war rations—everything from gasoline and coal to shoes and meat was allotted by coupon. Heeding the call to grow food at home, so farm produce could be delivered to the troops, the Davises planted vegetables in a backyard "victory garden" and potatoes on the front lawn. On their father's orders, Shelby and Diana got up early to pull weeds and to gather eggs from the chicken coop. Davis assumed the children enjoyed these rural chores; Kathryn informed him that they hated them. "Maybe," she said hopefully, "they'll like them better in 20 years when they have their own garden." Every Saturday, the family walked two miles along Route 9 to the neighboring town of Ossining, New York, to see a movie and eat ice cream cones. Kathryn left the car in the driveway. It was unpatriotic to waste gas when the military needed every gallon it could pump. It was also unpatriotic to leave drapes open if a room was lit at night. Americans shuttered their windows and darkened their yards so that enemy planes couldn't target populated areas. A beam of light shining through a window was a breach of "blackout" security, and neighbors were asked to report it to the local air raid warden.

For at-home entertainment, families gathered around a radio or a record player operated with a hand crank. The Davis's record player was installed in the upstairs bedroom, dubbed "the Davis Nightclub," where the children saw their parents dance and heard their first jazz albums. Downstairs, at the breakfast table, they formed a "barnyard orchestra," and brayed, oinked, clucked, mooed, bow-wowed, and baaed on cue. Shelby was the designated clucker. He liked chickens because he made a nice profit selling the eggs he gathered from the family chicken coop and sold with Diana. "We encouraged his door-to-door salesmanship," Kathryn recalls, "but we didn't realize he'd deplete our entire egg supply."

War in Europe tranquilized the New York Stock Exchange. Giddy buying in early 1939 ended in the fall, and a protracted decline followed. The popular theory that wars are bullish, based on the Dow's 1915 record advance, was disproved at the NYSE, which reached its 150th anniversary in a catatonic funk in 1942. On February 14 of that year, only 320,000 shares were bought and sold. It was a typically boring session; the trading floor resembled a lazy tropical resort. On August 19, 1940, the exchange had set a record for inactivity with only 129,650 shares traded—the lowest volume since 1916.*

World War II produced an industrial renaissance, just as Davis had predicted in his book. Once the United States entered the fray, stocks rallied. The Dow more than doubled from

---

*Several facts and figures cited in this chapter (the trading volume on the New York Stock Exchange, Joseph Schumpeter's bearish outlook, deflationary expectations for the late 1940s, the rise in federal spending during World War II, the Thomas Parkinson quote about "fictitious money," and the 34-year decline in bond prices) first appeared in James Grant's *The Trouble with Prosperity,* Times Business/Random House, 1996.

1942 to 1946. The government became the nation's biggest consumer. From steel to rubber to dry goods to munitions, companies retooled their factories to satisfy the only buyer that mattered: Uncle Sam. Among thousands of businesses given new life in the military retrofit was Art Loom. The looms were rebuilt to make uniforms instead of carpets, and the company's profits rose accordingly. Joe Wasserman had advised against "going overboard" on government contracts, but going overboard paid off, at least momentarily. Eventually, Art Loom was acquired by Mohawk, the largest carpet maker in the country.

To quell the inflation it had created, the Roosevelt Administration tried to control prices by rationing everything from wheat and sugar to nylon stockings. Consumers chafed at the restrictions and the government-induced austerity. Telephone workers struck for higher wages; coal miners, for meat. The wheat shortage begat a bread shortage, and the Roosevelt White House published the first official federal cookbook: *How to Make Bread-Free Lunches and Dinners*.

In 1944, Dewey returned to the New York governor's mansion, and he repaid Davis for his campaign work by naming him deputy superintendent in the state's insurance department. Davis could just as easily have been named deputy superintendent in the traffic department or the public relations office, but this chance appointment introduced him to the industry that would make his fortune.

He was assigned to the state's Manhattan outpost—a cluster of offices at 61 Broadway, on the outskirts of Wall Street. His ongoing mission was antibureaucratic: simplifying forms, streamlining procedures, revamping the accounting rules to make insurance reports easier to understand. He commuted between Manhattan and the rented cottage in Scarborough, but halfway through the first year, after Davis noticed irresistible bargains within commuting distance of Manhattan, Kathryn went house hunting.

A real estate agent showed her a three-story Colonial perched on three acres in Tarrytown. It had an unobstructed view of the Hudson River. The seller was a Mrs. Newberry, widow of the founder of a chain of five-and-ten-cent stores. Kathryn liked the river view but not the suburban neighborhood, and she knew Davis, given his druthers, would rather live on a farm. After Kathryn insisted she wasn't interested, the agent coaxed her into making a $5,000 offer. She was so sure of Mrs. Newberry's immediate rejection of this low-ball insult, she didn't bother to consult Davis before drawing up the contract.

Less than an hour later, the agent called with congratulations. Mrs. Newberry had accepted. "She decided to take a tax loss," Kathryn said. "When my husband came home that night, I told him we'd bought a house in Tarrytown. He cheered up when he heard the price. From then on, I was the designated house hunter for the family."

[Davis, who paid cash for his house, would soon be buying stocks with borrowed money (margin). After its losses in 1929 to 1932, the public disparaged margin investing, yet people routinely bought houses with margin loans, aka mortgages. Though they didn't think of mortgages this way, leverage in residential real estate was a main reason their houses gave them their biggest investment gains over the long term. Davis was confident that leverage applied to stocks was a far more potent profit booster than a mortgage, so he pursued the former and ignored the latter.]

Thus, the Davises became seat owners in 1941 and homeowners in 1945—the year when the surviving combatants came home from World War II, and the war rally in stocks was nearing its end. Even with the rally, the Dow and other major indexes sold below their 1929 prices. Potential investors were traumatized by fear of a depression encore, discouraged by the high taxes on dividend income (capital gains were taxed relatively modestly, but who had any?), and convinced

26

that peace was bad for business. Some expected the falling birthrate would subvert future prosperity (an idea advanced by economist Joseph Schumpeter). Most continued to favor the winning asset of the 1930s: bonds.

Davis didn't share the public's enthusiasm. Though bonds had won the decade, he realized that stocks were superior wealth producers. A stock was a slice of corporate ownership, and, if the company thrived, its upside was unlimited. A bondholder's reward was getting money back, plus interest, no matter how well a company fared. Moreover, though governments depended on bond sales to finance their activities, history showed that regimes of all types had subjected their loyal bondholders to inflationary practices, particularly during and after major wars. World War II was no exception. The war effort that had revitalized industry had been stunningly expensive. Costs ran far beyond the wildest estimates. In 1943, the government spent an abacus-warping $72 billion, which, thanks to the war tab, was $16 billion over budget. To put this in perspective, all the shares in all the companies listed on the New York Stock Exchange were worth only $36 billion. One year's federal outlay exceeded the market value of an all-star lineup of America's leading corporations by half.

There was a predictable hitch: The government lacked the funds to support the wartime spending spree. It solved the problem the old-fashioned way—by raising taxes, selling bonds, and printing fresh cash on federal presses. The strategy was classic: War debts were paid with cheap money, even though cheap money was inflationary. In a clumsy attempt to mollify investors, the Treasury Department put a "cap" on the interest it paid on its own bonds. Bond prices don't fall if interest rates don't rise, so bondholders were temporarily spared the losses that might have cooled their enthusiasm.

Davis became an antibond maverick. The recent past had told people bonds were attractive and safe, but the present was telling Davis they were ugly and dangerous. Interest rates were fast approaching what economist John Maynard Keynes called the "balm and sweet simplicity of no percent." Keynes was exaggerating, but not by much—the yield on long-term Treasuries hit bottom—2.03 percent—in April 1946. Buyers would have to wait 25 years to double their money, and, to Davis, this was pathetic compounding. He saw the threat in the "sea of money on which the U.S. Treasury has floated this costliest of wars." With the government deep in hock and forced to borrow another $70 billion to cover its latest shortfall, he was certain lenders soon would demand higher rates, not lower. The most reliable inflation gauge, the Consumer Price Index (CPI), rose sharply in 1946. Bond bulls turned a blind eye to the inflationary outbreak and ignored a basic lesson from Investment 101: Avoid bonds when the Consumer Price Index is rising. A second lesson—avoid bonds after a costly war—convinced Davis that the bonanza in government paper was over.

In the late 1920s, yesterday's proven winner was stocks, and the love-in for equities wrecked the net worth of a generation. A skeptical minority escaped into government bonds, a move that gave them an excellent and steady income for the next 17 years. Stocks never fully recovered. The late 1940s brought another turning point. By that time, bonds were yesterday's proven winners and were hailed as the safest and smartest investment. What followed was a 34-year bear market in bonds that lasted from the Truman era to the Reagan years. The 2 to 3 percent bond yields in the late 1940s expanded to 15 percent in the early 1980s, and, as yields rose, bond prices fell and bond investors lost money. The same government bond that sold for $101 in 1946 was worth only $17 in 1981! After three decades, loyal bondholders who had held their bonds lost 83 cents on every dollar they'd invested. Ignoring the scene in the rear-view mirror, Davis focused his attention on navigating the future.

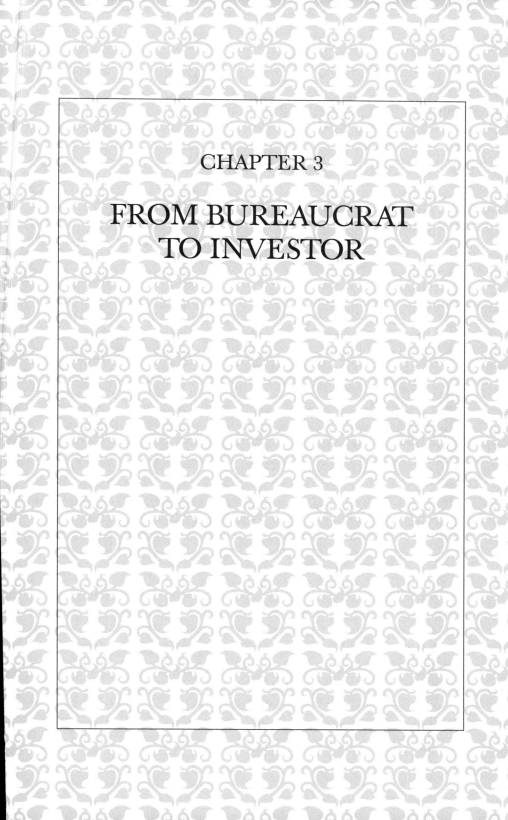

CHAPTER 3

FROM BUREAUCRAT TO INVESTOR

AVIS LEFT HIS STATE JOB FOR THE STOCK MARKET in 1947. Kathryn recalls her family's reaction to Davis's sudden exit from secure government work: "They thought it was a little crazy."

Bell Labs came out with the transistor that same year. Sony was born. Ajax, "the foaming cleanser," appeared on the shelves. "Cold War," a phrase coined by financier Bernard Baruch, entered the vocabulary. In a speech at Harvard, General George C. Marshall introduced his Marshall Plan to help Europe dig itself out of the rubble. Congress passed Taft-Hartley, a law designed to weaken labor unions. The first assembly-line houses were ready for occupancy in Levittown. Jackie Robinson broke the color line in baseball. The electric guitar made its debut. Stocks were still widely disparaged. The Dow stood—or reeled—at the 180 level, half off its 1929 high. Chemicals and autos hit new lows in 1946; rails and aircraft fell in 1947; and drugs and utilities went down a year later.

Investors faced the following choices. They could go the bond route, clip a 2.5 percent annual coupon for 30 years, and pay brutal taxes. Tax-free compounding [in IRAs, Keoghs, and 401(k) plans] hadn't been invented. The vast majority of Americans who couldn't afford bonds continued to store their liquid assets in savings accounts. In another example of how financial institutions were spared the rigors of the competitive free enterprise system they financed, all banks paid the same low-ball interest rates to depositors. The fix was in, imposed by the feds to guarantee bankers a source of cheap capital they could lend out at much higher rates, producing a favorable "spread." The wider the "spread," the greater a bank's margin of profit and safety, and the less chance it would fail. Bankers could worry less, keep bankers' hours (10:00 A.M. to 3:00 P.M., Monday through Friday), and play more golf.

Meanwhile, the interest paid to depositors, minus the taxes paid on the interest, didn't come close to beating inflation. That being the case, the savings account was guaranteed to deplete wealth. Year after year, dutiful savers lost money and rarely complained about it.

What about the stock route? Davis hadn't worked as an analyst for 10 years, but he'd kept up with developments. He knew stocks hadn't escaped the bargain basement. The Dow sold at 9.6 times earnings, only slightly above its book value. The average Dow company paid a 5 percent dividend, double what investors could get from Uncle Sam's bonds. Beyond the Dow, in almost every sector of the market, dividend yields far exceeded bond yields. On top of the yield, stockholders got the chance for capital gains.

Still, the public wasn't buying. Over 90 percent of the respondents to a Federal Reserve Board survey said they were opposed to the purchase of common stocks. As Davis put it, the masses held a "collective grudge against the market." The nation that fought and won the war to rid the earth of its biggest devils avoided the devil's money pit on Wall Street. The mutual fund industry, prominent in the 1920s, had all but

31

disappeared. Only 300,000 Americans owned shares in funds. Few people wanted to bet on American business, but Davis couldn't help noticing that business was on an upswing. American factories stood alone in the world—their foreign competitors had been obliterated in the war. Multinationals in the United States boosted their profits abroad by capturing European markets without resistance. Four former enemies—Italy, Austria, Germany, and Japan—became wards of the Allies. And America had the Bomb.

The release of postwar energy was more powerful than the Bomb. It cured the lingering Depression. Through the 1930s and into the 1940s, a mass market hardly existed in America. Restaurants, motels, and most stores were local. Nearly half of the nation's families earned less than $20 a week. They struggled to keep themselves fed, clothed, and sheltered. They emptied their wallets for necessities, with zilch left over for amenities. For these subsistence-level earners, "shop 'til you drop" was as alien a concept as surfing the Web.

Postwar prosperity brought what economists call "discretionary income" to millions of new retail customers who suddenly found themselves with cash for non-essential purchases. This extra cash had a fantastic multiplier effect. After a frustrating stretch of rationing and coupons, of regarding gasoline as an extravagance, butter and sugar as luxuries, meat as a treasure, and a new pair of nylons as an impossible dream, Americans exercised their freedom to shop. People bought everything and anything, and stretched the definition of "necessity" to include whatever caught their fancy.

Giddy with triumph and flush with separation pay, ex-GIs had more spending money in their pockets than any working-class population had ever amassed. They were acquiring houses, cars, and college degrees financed on the GI Bill. The housing boom led to a small appliances/home repairs/furnishings boom. The baby boom led to a diapers, laundry soap, pram, and crib boom. Nationwide, manufacturers thrived on the pent-up demand and switched quickly from a satisfy-Uncle-Sam mode to a satisfy-the-local-shopper mode. Cash registers from coast to coast merrily rang up sales, and gratified merchants added floor space and opened new stores. The economy kicked into high gear. Inflation was on the rise, but profits rose faster as improved machinery helped workers produce more goods per hour. Had Davis been assigned to the traffic department, the utility department, or the press office, he might have seen a great potential in auto stocks, electric companies, or newspaper stocks. But, as Peter Lynch would later advise, he specialized in what he understood—an industry that was overlooked by analysts and ignored by brokers.

Insurance was a trivial pursuit on Wall Street. Many insurance issues traded in the minor leagues of stock exchanges—the neighborhood stock parlors that comprised the "over-the-counter" market. As Davis had noticed, small stocks outran big stocks in the postwar era. He surmised the reason: Small companies could hike prices and control wages without "fear or threat of Congressional investigation or labor union pressure." In theory, the typical insurer enjoyed this advantage, but Davis was aware of a lingering absence of profit. Dow companies doubled their earnings from 1942 to 1947; fire insurers earned zilch. "The fire insurance industry is less profitable than at any time since the San Francisco fire [of 1906]," Davis said in one of his many speeches. "The rest of the business world has been feasting on the greatest bonanza America has ever seen. . . . My shirts cost more, my coal costs more, my bread costs more, my pork chops cost more. Practically everything I know of costs nearly twice as much as it did before the war—except fire insurance."

Davis blamed the earnings slump on low-yielding bonds held in insurers' portfolios. The industry got such a minimal payoff on its capital, it had trouble setting aside the necessary "reserves" to cover future claims from policyholders. "Typi-cally, the biggest problem for a life insurance company is sell-ing policies," Davis told a group of industry leaders in 1946: "Today, the bigger problem is [how to invest] the proceeds."

Though the lack of earnings was superficially disturbing, Davis was convinced not only that stocks in general had a prodigious upside, but insurance stocks offered extreme re-ward at minimal risk. Without formal CPA training, Davis had learned the quirks of insurance accounting—designed to satisfy state regulators, not inform potential investors. Like a gold miner who wore rags to the claims office to avoid calling attention to his lucky strike, the industry presented itself in as poor a light as possible. When an agent sold a new policy, the commission was 120 percent of the first month's payment. Thus, each new sale created a loss on paper.

Davis devised various rules of thumb to compensate for this and other anomalies. The typical insurer, he discovered, was selling for less than "book value." The bonds and mort-gages held in its fixed-income portfolio were worth far more than the market price of the company's own shares. Any buyer of those shares got his or her money's worth—and then some—in a slice of the portfolio. As a bonus, the buyer got the ongoing insurance business thrown in for free, and as if that weren't enough, the buyer received the annual 4 to 5 percent dividend, or double the yield on the beloved long-term Trea-sury bond.

With a bit of pencil pushing, the tangibles and intangibles could be assessed. Underneath the drab earnings, the insurers' portfolios were merrily compounding, as bond interest and mortgage payments rolled in. In his earlier role, Davis hadn't differentiated compounding machines from other types of companies, but the regulatory job had taught him this crucial distinction. Where manufacturers expended capital to devise a salable product, then spent more to upgrade their factories and improve the merchandise, insurers took in cash from every new customer and spent belatedly, when claims were filed or policies matured.

Bonds and mortgages in the insurers' possession were bought with customers' money. Assuming unexpected claims didn't deplete the portfolio, an insurer could amass a gigantic hidden asset that someday would belong to the shareholders. Patient investors could wait for the hidden asset to grow, expect other investors to discover it, and then bid up the price. Other people's installment payments, plus interest, then became their own life savings instead.

This shareholder alchemy required no boiling cauldrons, potions, amulets, or magic words. Any stock picker could benefit, and the how-to aspects of so-called "value investing" were fully described in Ben Graham's *Securities Analysis,* first published in 1934. Graham resolved the popular confusion between speculating and investing by arguing that stockholders could be investors or speculators, depending on what they bought and how much they paid for it. Graham advised buying shares in businesses that were selling for less than the liquidation value of the assets. That way, the chances of losing money were drastically reduced. People who looked for a payoff at minimal risk were investing. People who paid silly prices for the unrealized potential of celebrated upstarts in promising but unproven endeavors were speculating.

Although he was a nonentity to the general public, Graham had a cult following among the actuarial cognoscenti. His most ardent disciple was Warren Buffett, but Davis also had studied Graham's writings and admired his ideas. In 1947, Davis was elected president of Graham's stock analysts' organization.

On top of their allure as value players, insurance companies benefited from a surge in the demand for policies. Newlyweds with new houses and new cars in the driveway needed three kinds of coverage: life, home, and auto. The lead story in the July 1948 issue of Kiplinger's magazine, the *Changing Times,* caught Davis's attention. It was entitled: "What a Young Man Should Do with His Money." The first bit of advice: "Start by buying at least $20,000 of life insurance." A decade earlier, one-third of the nation's savings had been tied up in life insurance; in the 1940s, that percentage increased. War had been bullish for insurance agents. Record sales were reported after the attack on Pearl Harbor. Customers bought more policies and faithfully paid the premiums. "Lapses" (the industry's euphemism for nonpayment) and "surrenders" (some people simply gave up their policies) hit all-time lows in the 1940s. By 1944, 159 million policies were in force nationwide; nearly 16 million of them belonged to military personnel. GIs who took out insurance for five years were persuaded to convert to 20-year policies. Davis noted another boon for the industry: the "bull market in longevity." When it came to dying, policyholders were taking their time. They were alive and paying premiums—as opposed to dead, with their heirs collecting on their policies. Insurers, Davis said, were "growth companies in disguise"—growing like crazy but "people don't think of it that way." Electric utilities fit the same category in the 1950s. Much later, Davis's son found disguised growth opportunities in consumer companies in the 1980s and financial companies in the 1990s.

The more he learned about the industry he regulated, the more Davis was convinced he'd stumbled onto a mother lode. In case after case, he found companies selling for less than book value, paying hefty dividends, and offering superior long-term compounding. With his boss and mentor the odds-on favorite to win the presidency in 1948, Davis could have hung on Dewey's coattails, expecting to ride them to Washington. But a chance at a high-level Washington job didn't interest him as much as the insurance business. If the companies he regulated couldn't be persuaded to put more common stocks in their portfolios, at least he could show the world at large why they should put insurance stocks in theirs. To that end, he submitted his resignation.

To gain a base of operations, Davis bought a controlling interest in Frank Brokaw & Co., which advertised itself as the "oldest specialist in insurance stocks." Brokaw had been pounding the table for his favorite insurers since the 1930s. Bad timing undid him, and his firm was on the ropes. Davis decided he could benefit from Brokaw's staying power by keeping the "oldest specialist" tag, erasing "Brokaw," and re-naming the enterprise Shelby Cullom Davis & Co. His seat on the New York Stock Exchange came in handy. It gave him access to the trading floor and a license to do business alongside the big-league Wall Street houses. His was now a "member firm" with all rights and privileges attached. Davis allowed Brokaw to stay on as his partner, at least temporarily, but several months into the new arrangement, Brokaw dissolved the partnership by drowning in the Atlantic Ocean. The coroners ruled his death a suicide.

Davis now had the office to himself. It was located at 110 William Street, just off Wall Street—the financial equivalent of off-Broadway. It contained twin desks and two black phones. The phone number (in May 1948) was Beekman 3-0626. Kathryn served as the in-house answering service. "It was easy work," she recalls, "but boring. Nobody called. I sat there reading a book."

In the country at large, wartime austerity had given way to peacetime spending, but in the Davis household, austerity was still in effect. The resident stock picker emerged from his bedroom at 6:00 A.M., cooked his own breakfast on a hot plate in the bathroom, ate while he dressed, dressed without noticing what he was wearing, grabbed his briefcase, and called for Kathryn to drive him to the train station. He caught the 7:00 A.M. commuter from Tarrytown to New York. His neighbors opted for the 8:00 A.M. club car, which gave them more time to sleep and a cushier ride. Davis preferred an earlier start and nobody to bother him while he read the *Wall Street Journal*. He also liked getting a jump on the Wall Street crowd. The lower fare at 7:00 A.M. was a bonus.

As a member of the private sector, Davis addressed the Insurance Accountants Association at the Hotel New Yorker on May 12, 1948. "My topic today is close not only to the hearts but indeed to the very lives of those who look to fire insurance for sustenance," he said, as if he were facing a roomful of heroic fighters instead of pencil-pushing Dilberts. His speeches were heavily salted with "very," "indeed," and "I need not remind you," as in: "This is a great industry, I need not remind you, one of the oldest and most honorable in America. . . ."

He described how policyholders weren't the only people who benefited from a robust insurance industry. A "large and silent body" of shareholders—including universities, hospitals, missionaries, and others—had invested part of their savings in insurance stocks. "They all suffered when regulators rejected rate increases and squashed industry profits." More profit, he thundered, meant more jobs and more prosperity at large.

During 1947 and 1948, he'd crisscrossed the country several times, pounding the table for insurance stocks. He delivered the pitch to foundations, pension funds, and wealthy individuals, just as his drowned partner had done, with minimal success, a decade earlier. He expected that whoever bought shares on his recommendation would let him handle the trades, and he could pocket the commissions. "Would you buy Standard Oil at half today's price?" he asked his audiences. The crowd always hollered "Yes!" Insurance stocks, he enthused, offered them the same discount. The typical insurer was selling for half the value of its captured assets. This, he said, was "the greatest fire sale in history."

"I myself have been battering against the doors," Davis admitted, describing the effort to raise capital for seven insurers about to go public. His firm was the smallest of several syndicates involved in this underwriting. He expected his coast-to-coast road show to rouse buyers, but it didn't. "Apparently," Davis snorted, "the horny-handed savers of this country will not pay one plugged nickel for those assets. . . ."

One of the new public offerings was Aetna. Existing shareholders had first dibs on the shares, but took only half their allotment. Davis and his cohorts in the other syndicates struggled to unload the remainder.

"Why, under such circumstances . . . did I not have to beat off would-be purchasers with a club?" Davis asked—and then answered his own question. First, stocks were still anathema to most people. President Harry S. Truman had lampooned Wall Street so gleefully during the 1948 campaign that his victory caused Charles Merrill, founder of Merrill Lynch, to take out newspaper ads to rebut the President's attack.

"Mr. Truman knows as well as anybody: There isn't any Wall Street," scoffed Merrill. "That's just legend. Wall Street is Montgomery Street in San Francisco. Seventeenth Street in Denver. Marietta Street in Atlanta. Federal Street in Boston. Main Street in Waco, Texas. And it's any spot in Independence, Missouri, where thrifty people go to invest their money, to buy and sell securities."

Would-be purchasers had given Davis the following reasons not to buy his favorite insurers: (1) Wars cause a "general loosening of morals." Returning GIs will set fires and burglarize their neighbors. Insurance companies will be stuck with the bill. (2) Insurers had recently paid a whopping claim from an explosion at a nitrate plant that killed 576 people in Texas City, Texas, in 1947. Another mega-disaster might put them out of business. (3) The oft-predicted atomic warfare was an insurance nightmare. Imagine the claims from World War III! (4) Nuclear power plants would leave a radioactive mess, causing another huge insurance tab.

The frustrating road-show flop was a blessing in disguise. In the *Intelligent Investor,* a sequel to his famous *Securities Analysis,* Benjamin Graham had written: "[To] enjoy a reasonable chance of continued better-than-average results, the investor must follow policies which are (1) inherently sound and promising, and (2) are not popular on Wall Street." Davis devoted his new career to this two-part maxim. If shortsighted audiences ignored his recommendations, he'd take his own advice. His underwriting and brokerage operations quickly became secondary to his own portfolio. He turned his attention to buying sound and promising companies in this unpopular industry.

Investing through his licensed firm gave him two key advantages over the typical neighborhood stock picker: (1) he could buy more shares on margin because the SEC gave firms more leeway to borrow money than it gave individuals, and (2) a firm paid a lower rate of interest. A large crowd of unwary enthusiasts had bought stocks on margin and lost their life savings in 1929, but Davis was comfortable borrowing the maximum the SEC allowed—slightly more than 50 percent. Unlike his hapless predecessors, who bought stocks at sucker prices on margin, he figured the cut-rate prices for insurance companies gave him a safety net.

"My father hated taxes," says Shelby, "so margin became his favorite weapon against the IRS. The interest he paid on his loans was tax-deductible, and his deductions wiped out the taxes he'd otherwise have owed on the dividends he got. Also, by raising the stakes on his investing, margin kept him focused."

Davis continued to travel widely—not so much to tout companies to others, but to analyze them for himself. He visited CEOs in Hartford and elsewhere, quizzing them on recent results and plans for the future. Face-to-face meetings helped him separate the "bluffers from the doers." Today's Wall Street analysts make corporate house calls as a matter of course; Davis pioneered the practice. CEOs routinely announced goals for the future. Davis challenged them to provide details. It turned him off when a company made definitive predictions about its long-term profit growth but was vague on how it planned to achieve it. One of Davis's favorite questions was: "If you had one silver bullet to shoot a competitor, which competitor would you shoot?" He'd get the answer, and make a note to research the competitor's stock. A company that was feared by its rivals must be doing something right. "Meeting with my partners," he called these fact-finding forays; since history taught him great civilizations are built by great leaders, he looked for great leadership in executive suites.

Once he had opened his firm, Davis sought out Graham, Warren Buffett's professor at Columbia University. Graham was on a mission to transform stock analysis from a rustic craft to a serious profession. To that end, Graham lobbied for better training and certification for Wall Street's bean counters, and more reliable accounting from public companies. His efforts led to the creation of the New York Society of Security Analysts (NYSSA), which, by the mid-1940s, had attracted 1,000 members.

Davis joined the NYSSA to drum up business and to support Graham's campaign. At this point, analysts were low-pay, low-profile, and low-priority people on Wall Street. They did research for institutional clients (pension funds, among others) but had minimal contact with the public.

Meanwhile, Davis's early stock picks were merrily compounding. He'd started his fledgling company with $100,000 in assets ($50,000 cash plus the seat on the NYSE, valued at $50,000). By the end of year one, his net worth was pegged at $234,790. Seven insurance stocks gave him the kind of liftoff that today's investors might associate with high-tech names.

His biggest holding was a relatively large insurer, Crum & Forster (later absorbed by Xerox). The others were smaller and obscure. They traded in the financial boondocks known as the over-the-counter market, and increased sales and profits at a Microsoftian clip.

While the Dow went south (down 24 percent from 1947 to 1949), Davis's portfolio went north. He was in the right stocks and the right industry, and his rapid moneymaking got a considerable boost from leverage. He borrowed $29,000 the first year and continued to borrow to the maximum throughout his career. For unknown reasons, trace amounts of U.S. Steel and United Air Lines "preferred" shares appeared in his holdings. Plenty of money managers would have advised him to buy more of the world's mightiest steel maker and less of the mom-and-pop underwriters. But he stuck to his plan and invested strategically rather than nostalgically. Nostalgia for America's smokestack heavyweights was hazardous to wealth: U.S. Steel stock topped out in 1954 and then began a 40-year descent.

CHAPTER 4

WALL STREET A GO-GO

I N THE SUMMER OF 1965, FED CHAIRMAN William McChesney Martin spoke of "disquieting similarities between our present prosperity and the fabulous Twenties." Martin elaborated as follows: "Then as now, many government officials, scholars and businessmen were convinced that a new economic era had opened, an era in which business fluctuations had become a thing of the past, in which poverty was about to be abolished, and in which perennial economic progress and expansion were assured."

Martin's misgivings were ignored as the Dow slogged toward the magic 1000 pinnacle. Though the most dyspeptic fortune-teller wouldn't have predicted such an uninspiring future performance, Dow 1000 wasn't exceeded for good until the early 1980s. A sharp but abbreviated decline in 1966, precipitated when U.S. planes bombed Hanoi, was a warm-up for trouble ahead. The Fed raised rates twice, and a credit crunch stalled the home builders. The Dow wheezed to a geriatric halt. President Lyndon Johnson demanded that G.K. Funston, president of NYSE, and SEC Chairman Manuel F. Cohen do something about falling prices—as if the trend could be reversed by decree.

Many non-Dow stocks raced ahead, as so-called "go-go" investors jumped on hot issues for a quick lift. Go-go mutual funds (more on these in a minute) posted gains of 40 percent or better in 1965, thanks to "new era" companies like Applied Logic; nursing-home chains that stood to benefit from Medicare (Four Seasons Nursing centers, United Convalescent Homes), and aggressive fast-food outfits such as Kentucky Fried Chicken. If you bought (and held) Fairchild Camera in early 1965, you tripled your money in four years. If you bought Boise Cascade in early 1967, you quadrupled your money in two years. If you bought blue chips, your portfolio went nowhere.

Sluggish blue chips, in the face of vigorous public buying, meant veteran shareholders were vigorously selling. A mass transfer of assets from the smart money crowd to the naïve money crowd was called "distribution." Never was there more spirited and widespread distribution than in the era of drugs, free love, and rock-and-roll. The floor of the New York Stock Exchange was roused from its lassitude. Two million shares changed hands during a typical session in the 1950s; 10 to 12 million shares traded daily in the late 1960s. On June 13, 1968, a 21-million-share day caused the NYSE to choke on its paperwork and shut down operations. As Wall Street reveled in hyperactivity, U.S. cities burned in summer race riots. "The great garbage market," one pundit called the final buying spree in the twilight of the second great bull market of the century. Merrill Lynch opened 200,000 new accounts in five months in 1969.

Americans had flipped over mutual funds, which now controlled $35 billion in client assets, 35 times more than they'd handled a generation earlier. One quarter of the value of all stock transactions was effected by fund managers. An appealing aspect of funds was their apparent buoyancy in a market undertow, as they'd exhibited in the 1962 sell-off. Alas, one triumph didn't make a trend, as subsequent undertows would reveal.

Go-go managers, also known as gunslingers, jumped on smaller issues that shot up the fastest, and then jumped off as soon as the prices stopped rising. They bought high-tech wonders and quickly replaced them with higher-tech wonders. A long-term investment lingered in the portfolio a few weeks. Gunslinging Gerry Tsai, a Fidelity defector who launched his own Manhattan Fund, became America's first celebrity stock jockey. At his Fifth Avenue corporate bivouac, Tsai reportedly kept the thermostat at 55 degrees Fahrenheit to "keep his head clear." The press played him as inscrutable and suggested that his Oriental background gave him a built-in knack for sage investing. Where Tsai had hoped to raise $25 million, he ended up with $247 million.

Fred Alger cowed the competition and wowed the public with his Security Equity Fund in New York. On the West Coast, ex-broker Fred Carr of the Enterprise Fund mixed the past with the future by filling his office with antique furniture and op art. Carr's investing was more op-arty than antiquated: He bought flashy start-ups that most of his colleagues had never heard of. In May 1969, *Business Week* flattered Carr by saying he "may just be the best portfolio manager in the U.S." Another Fred, Fred Mates, weighed in with a buy-no-evil approach in 1967. The Mates Fund portfolio kept itself free of military contractors, cigarette companies, and polluters, so clients could make a guilt-free return. Mates called his staff the "flower children." After a year in operation, the feel-good fund caused clients to feel even better, with a 168 percent gain. Mates closed the sales window to keep from being overwhelmed with cash, clients, and paperwork. To "make poor people rich," he planned to offer a minimum investment of only $50 and market his product in urban ghettos and other disadvantaged areas.

By 1969, mutual funds controlled $50 billion worth of stock and were replacing their inventory at a rate of 50 percent a year, a frenetic pace when compared to the 20 percent turnover in 1962. Taking a cue from the professionals, fund clients switched funds as readily as managers switched their holdings. Fund surfing was in vogue, and investors moved in and out of top performers, trying to catch the latest wave. The surfers paid big commissions at every turn, but if a Mates or a Carr could double their money in a year, who cared?

As go-go was about to become no-go, an obscure but extremely rewarding money manager and New Era disbeliever named Warren Buffett quietly distinguished himself with a non-go-go portfolio. Investors in his private partnership enjoyed a 59 percent gain in 1968, while the Dow rose a mediocre 9 percent. Having triumphed on the upside, Buffett shocked his financial peer group by doing the unthinkable. He liquidated his investments and sent back his partners' money, along with a letter informing them that his supply of "promising ideas" had been exhausted; with stocks selling at Tiffany prices, he could find nothing promising to buy. He parked his own assets in boring municipal bonds. A shortage of promising ideas didn't stop Wall Street experts from continuing to recommend the priciest issues. Merrill Lynch flogged IBM at 39 times earnings; Bache pushed Xerox at 50 times earnings; Blair & Company touted Avon at 56 times earnings. McGeorge Bundy, president of the Ford Foundation, needled his fellow fiduciaries for being too conservative with their endowments and trusts, and urged them to throw money at stocks.

In a frenzied search for the "next Xerox," investors bought shares in anything with "electronic" or "data processing" in its name. Companies bought each other just as readily, and Wall

Street played host to merger madness. Clumsy conglomerates such as ITT, Litton, and Ling-Temco-Vought got bigger and clumsier. Davis wouldn't have touched such stocks, but, as you'll see Shelby did.

In 1968, a giddy Mr. Market had high-stepped over and around the Martin Luther King and Robert Kennedy assassinations, jack-booted cops pummeling protesters at the Democratic national convention in Chicago, widespread campus riots, and foreign banks shunning the dollar. As John Brooks wrote, "The silly market had gone its merry way, heedlessly soaring upward as if everything were okay. . . ."

"A new-issues craze is always the last stage of a dangerous boom," noted Brooks, and, in 1969, new issues abounded. The most popular of these debutantes were called "shooters" because their prices shot up, often doubling during the first day of trading. Nursing homes and other health-care issues that expected to benefit from Medicare were standouts in the shooting range.

In spite of the cult of personality that developed around the go-go managers, a study of the 1960 to 1968 period, published by the Twentieth Century Fund, concluded that blindly buying the market at large was more rewarding than paying a professional to pick the stocks. It was a moot point. Soon after this study appeared in 1969, the rewards vanished. A three-month drubbing left the Dow clinging to 800 points by the spring of 1970. Economists were confounded by the coexistence of inflation and recession, which they called stagflation. The country had sunk into a grand funk—"one of the deepest moods of gloom to darken any American April since the Civil War," said Brooks.

Vanishing assets were as much effect as cause, though a lingering Vietnam War, bloodier campus riots (four Kent State University students were killed by Ohio National Guardsmen), and upheaval along the racial fault line contributed. A venerable railroad, Penn Central, collapsed in bankruptcy. The dollar sank lower, and home builders were idled; on Wall Street, 100 firms faced extinction or merger. The NYSE motto, "Own your share in American business," was dropped without explanation. By May 1970, Brooks reported, "A portfolio consisting of one share of every stock listed on the Big Board was worth just about half what it would have been worth at the start of 1969."

As usual, the high flyers fell harder than the Dow, which was down 36 percent. Investors who owned overhyped stocks like Data Processing, Control Data, Electronic Data Systems, or anything else with "data" in its name, did worse. Ten prominent conglomerates lost an average of 86 percent apiece; tech stocks in general lost 77 percent; and computer leasing stocks lost 80 percent. The computerized Nasdaq market made its debut in 1970, just in time for Nasdaq-type stocks to wreak havoc.

As performance stocks underachieved, so did the gunslingers who owned them. Gerry Tsai had timed his exit well. Two years earlier, in the nowhere market of 1968, his Manhattan Fund earned a minus 6 percent, dropping his ranking to 299th among 305 competing funds. Tsai promptly sold his company for $30 million-plus and retired from active management. He wasn't around to take the real punishment.

The Freds stayed in business long enough to ruin their reputations and traumatize their clients. Fred Carr's Enterprise Fund lost half its value. Carr resigned nine months after he was lauded in *Business Week*. At least he had the consolation of having kept up with the dartboard; the typical stock on the NYSE was cut in half as well. To stop frantic shareholders from fleeing his fund, Fred Mates persuaded the SEC to let him freeze the fund's assets. This was a controversial maneuver at best, and the Omega fiasco made it worse. Mates had bought a large block of "restricted shares" in that company.

There was a required waiting period before the shares could be sold on the open market. Many funds trafficked in restricted issues, paying a low price and carrying the shares on the books at a much higher price, creating instant gratification. For example, having bought the restricted version of Omega for $3.25, Mates put a $16 valuation on his purchase. This "gain" helped his fund rise to the top of the performance charts in 1968.

A year later, when $16 Omega had lost its plausibility, a crowd of Mates's clients rushed to exit his portfolio. With Omega restricted, Mates had trouble selling the quantity of stock needed to raise enough cash to reimburse the defectors. That's when he appealed to the SEC to halt the reimbursement.

By the time he was ready to accommodate the defectors, Omega was a 50-cent product, and Mr. Market had depreciated considerably. Mates had hoped stocks would rally and his clients would rethink their decision to quit his portfolio, but stocks didn't rally and the clients didn't rethink. Eventually, the Mates Fund lost 90 percent of its former self.

Overpriced insurance issues weren't spared the markdown. Like most stocks, their lofty valuations weren't supportable, and their decline was accompanied by a barrage of negative publicity. A *Fortune* magazine reporter and a respected statistician both wrote convincingly that insurance had been a lousy business all along.

The statistician was Dr. Irving Plotkin. In 1968, this nervy 26-year-old ruffled the industry with a well-researched study that covered most of the period in which Davis had built his insurance portfolio: 1955 to 1968. Plotkin showed how insurers earned far less on their investment dollar than other types of companies earned on theirs. Not only were insurance earnings skimpy, they also were volatile and swung wildly from one season to the next.

One reason for the low profits was the tight regulatory collar under which all insurers chafed. Companies endlessly sought permission to charge more for their products, and regulators routinely refused to grant it. In the regulators' view, insurers had squirreled away heaps of valuable assets in their portfolios, so they could afford to charge less and give their customers a break. In the insurers' view, their assets were constantly threatened by escalating claims and future disasters. A case in point was auto insurance, a main subject of the *Fortune* cover piece that hit the stands in December 1970: "Why Nobody Likes the Insurers." Since the late 1950s, according to the reporter, Jeremy Main, the cost of insuring a car had risen twice as fast as the cost of living. In spite of this apparent windfall, the typical insurance company struggled.

According to Main, the entire property/casualty sector had lost a cumulative $1.5 billion since 1955, a year of record profits. This chronic underachievement, said Main, was caused by dull management, too many agents feeding at the commission trough, and a litigious population.

These well-publicized negatives made Davis's accomplishment all the more impressive. How did an apparently lousy industry provide an exceptional reward to the astute investor? There were several reasons. Insurers hid their true profitability, so the aforementioned lack of profit may have been, at least in part, an actuarial illusion. Davis bought when insurers were cheap, especially the mom-and-pop kind in his original portfolio. When these small companies were acquired by bigger companies, Davis reaped a windfall. He caught the post-World War II boom in home, auto, and life insurance policies. He avoided investing in chronic underachievers—Aetna, for example—that punished shareholder loyalty. He sought out aggressive, low-cost compounding machines like the Japanese insurers, Berkshire Hathaway, and AIG, which steadily enhanced shareholder value for decades. A well-managed technology company could always be toppled by a clever competitor or the latest scientific eureka from a rival. A well-managed insurer could outfox and outlast the competition, and never had to worry about becoming obsolete.

CHAPTER 5

SHELBY AND NEW YORK VENTURE FUND

I N 1969, THE YEAR WHEN NEIL ARMSTRONG strolled on the moon in his Michelin suit, the Davis era gave way to the Shelby era. The dividing line is somewhat arbitrary. Shelby already had been working on Wall Street, and Davis's investing career was only half over. But Shelby, along with sidekick Jeremy Biggs, took charge of the New York Venture Fund in 1969. For the first time, Shelby was picking stocks in the public arena and being audited by the SEC. Davis wasn't around to witness his son's debut. He'd left the country for an ambassadorial appointment in Switzerland. President Richard Nixon had offered the post, and Secretary of State William Rogers, a Davis crony since the Dewey days, brokered the deal.

Davis, at age 60, was the beneficiary of 20 uplifting years. This entire stretch had been fruitless to bondholders and fruitful to stockholders of all stripes. It was hard *not* to make money on equities. During this extraordinary run, the Dow was up fivefold while Dow earnings had merely doubled. The gains had depended on the public's willingness to pay escalating prices for earnings. Investors' presumption regarding future corporate profit had boosted stock prices more than actual corporate profit. Moreover, the actual profit was enhanced by borrowed money; corporate debt expanded fivefold over the 20-year period.

Years before, Davis couldn't have started investing at a better moment. He got in when the buying public was distrustful and stocks had nowhere to go but up; Shelby couldn't have begun the New York Venture Fund at a worse moment. He entered in the thin air of valuation, when the public was euphoric and prices were fantastical. Davis started investing in a sweet spot: the typical stock sold at six times earnings and carried an 8 to 10 percent dividend; interest rates were low; and a Treasury bond paid less than 3 percent. Shelby started investing for the Fund in a sour spot: stocks were selling at 20 to 25 times earnings and carried a 3 to 4 percent dividend; and a Treasury bond was paying 5 to 6 percent. The aging bull was in its death throes. The Dow had hit a top it wouldn't see again for another 15 years. The immediate future was treacherous for bondholders *and* for stockholders. Being out of bonds or stocks was more rewarding than being in them. Gold and the lowly money market triumphed in the early years of Shelby's tenure. He had entered at the most dangerous entry point since 1929.

Returning to the scene of their courtship, Davis and Kathryn moved into the ambassador's manse in Bern. Davis was delighted to serve in a country full of tightwads like himself, where insurance was a glamour industry. Refusing to let a sleeping asset lie, Davis rented the family house in Tarrytown. One month's rental income exceeded what the Davises had paid for the place three decades earlier.

Swiss diplomats were amazed at Davis's knack for remembering names. At one gathering after another, he stood up and introduced every person in the room without consulting the guest list. His experience at the patriotic societies' functions—wearing sashes and medallions, presiding at ceremonial dinners—served him well in Bern.

For his ambassadorial garb, Davis upgraded to tailored suits and high-end shoes. "I'm representing my country," he told his wife, justifying his sartorial reformation. Every day, at public functions, he wore a red carnation in his lapel. "One person is sure to miss me when I leave Switzerland," he joked. "The person who provides the flowers." He assumed they were plucked from the ambassadorial garden, but near the end of his tenure was annoyed to discover the embassy bought them at a store. Had he known earlier, he would have dispensed with this "waste of taxpayers' money."

Davis left his second-in-command, Ken Ebbitt, to run the office in New York and to baby-sit his portfolio. Ebbitt was a bond trader and had no feel for stocks, but his boss wasn't overly concerned. The ambassador immersed himself in his duties: improving Swiss-American relations and coaxing Swiss bankers to abolish secret accounts where the world's biggest crooks stashed their ill-gotten gains. His aversion to capital gains taxes kept him from selling holdings back home, so he was fully invested for the wealth reduction to come. Being out of the country didn't stop the losses, but it removed him from the tumult and the fallout, the finger-pointing and the despair the bears soon would bring to Wall Street.

Shelby had prepared for his opportunity—such as it was—his entire pre- and postadolescent life. A self-taught investor, Davis had cobbled together his maxims and his modus operandi from a variety of experiences and sources. Shelby had the whole program hammered into him from the start. Shelby's childhood was his MBA. He'd grown up on dinner-table stock talk, fact-finding missions to Hartford, and annual reports strewn about the house. He absorbed finance the way a musician's child absorbs syncopation or the diatonic scale.

From the time he was 9 or so, Shelby and his sister Diana, then 7½, served as their father's part-time clerical department. "If you work hard," Davis told the children, "maybe you'll get to like it." Every other Sunday afternoon, they cranked out copies of Davis's biweekly insurance letter on the office mimeograph, collated pages, stuffed and sealed envelopes, and affixed stamps.

"Dear Fiduciary," each letter began. The children wondered what a fiduciary was. They also wondered whether anybody read the letter, and why they weren't getting paid in cash, instead of in dinners at local restaurants. "Better than my cooking," Kathryn said, but the children would have preferred cash.

Shelby was coached on the basics of investing. Around the dinner tables of America, circa 1950, families traded opinions on the McCarthy hearings, the Korean War, the invincible New York Yankees. In parks and backyards, other fathers taught sons the three balls: base, basket, and foot. Davis taught his son about insurance companies: how they paid claims, what could ruin them, how they grew their assets. His passion was infectious.

Along with the popular homilies of the day—"Honesty is the best policy," "A penny saved is a penny earned," and so on, Shelby learned more sophisticated lessons of business and finance:

- Don't be a bondholder. Bondholders are lenders. Be a shareholder. Shareholders are owners. Owning shares in a successful company is far more rewarding than owning its bonds.
- The more wisely you invest, the faster your bankroll will expand. If you know the rate of return on your investment,

the Rule of 72 tells you how long it will take to double your money. The greater the return, the faster the compounding, which is why an extra percent or two makes a huge difference. A 10 percent return over 21½ years turns $100,000 into $400,000. At 12 percent, the payoff is $595,509.

In the summer of 1950, the Davises had driven west on the Pennsylvania Turnpike. Their destination was Springfield, Illinois, headquarters of Franklin Life Insurance. Franklin Life didn't attract many tourists, but visiting an insurance company was Davis's idea of a good time. On separate trips, he'd taken the family to the home offices of Glens Falls Insurance in Glens Falls, New York; Lincoln National in Fort Wayne, Indiana; and Businessmen's Assurance in Des Moines, Iowa. Usually, Kathryn and the children killed time in local parks and museums while Davis hobnobbed in boardrooms with CEOs and CFOs, reviewing future plans and critiquing past performance. Upon arriving at each corporate enclave, Davis checked the executive parking lot for empty spaces—evidence that the leadership might be working harder to improve a golf score than to increase the return on shareholders' capital.

He also liked to nose around the hallways and waiting rooms, looking for signs of waste, inefficiency, designer furniture, and other expensive froufrou. Shelby, at age 13, had sat in on an interview at Franklin Life. Looking around at the high ceilings, dark wood paneling, and gilded trim, he decided there was a lot of money in this place. The same thought, "That's where the money is," launched Willie Sutton's career as a bank robber. If only Sutton had been taught the Davis method of extracting wealth by owning shares, the quotable felon could have spared himself a lot of jail time. In any event, Franklin Life impressed Shelby enough that he bought shares with his own money. This was the first stock he ever owned, and the price increased tenfold before Franklin was bought out by American Tobacco in the 1980s.

The Springfield trip was also Shelby's introduction to the downside of stocks. In the June swelter, as the family cruised the Pennsylvania Turnpike with the radio on, they heard President Harry Truman (the surprise winner over Davis's ex-boss, Thomas E. Dewey, in the 1948 race for the White House) declare war on North Korea. Stock prices dropped after Truman's announcement. It was the first notable reversal since Davis had started his firm, yet he seemed to welcome the sell-off. "Out of crisis comes opportunity," Shelby remembers him saying. "A down market lets you buy more shares in great companies at favorable prices. If you know what you're doing, you'll make most of your money from these periods. You just won't realize it until much later."

The Davises rented a cottage in a Maine summer colony—Northeast Harbor—far beyond the commuter lines, and a 10-hour drive from Manhattan. By the mid-1950s, they'd bought their own vacation home on a ridge above the village. Built by a Cabot (from Boston) railroad magnate, the rambling wooden retreat provided a magnificent view of the harbor and the ocean beyond.

Except for this real estate purchase, the family's escalating net worth had no noticeable effect on the household budget or routine. Around the house, Davis wore moth-eaten sweaters and tattered pants. On family hikes, he led the way with his soles flapping. When Kathryn tossed the old shoes out, he'd rescue them from the trash, reattach the soles with glue, tape, or rubber bands, and return them to the closet. One summer, the family's hired cook reported a gas smell coming from the old stove, which was so rusty that metal flakes sometimes fell into the food. Poking at a rust hole below the main burner, she suggested her boss buy a new stove. Davis sniffed the air around the burner and patted the ancient appliance. "We don't need a new stove," he insisted. "Just paint the old one."

Kathryn knew the money was piling up but, to her, paper wealth was a mirage. The summer house, the airlift from Maine to Wall Street, and Davis's obvious delight with his career change signaled prosperity, but at a time when millionaires were scarce and didn't live next door, the children had no clue their father had become one. There were no plans to abandon the main residence in Tarrytown—their Sparta in the suburbs—for more elegant digs. The family drove an economical Chevy, flew tourist, and stayed in cut-rate lodges on ski trips. The children weren't allowed to order lobster in restaurants. The only lobster they ate was bought in fish stores or at the local dock in Maine.

Davis passed along his conviction that frugality was more than idle virtue. In his view, a dollar spent was a dollar wasted; a dollar unspent could be sent off to compound. He taught the children not to squander pecuniary resources. At home or on the road, they treated money the way desert tribes treat water—using as little as possible for any given task. Inside an investment account, which was where it belonged, money was a joyous and nourishing substance. Outside an investment account, in the hands of spenders, money was worrisome and potentially toxic. It sapped self-reliance and subverted the work urge of its possessors.

From chats with their peers, the Davis children discovered that they got smaller allowances and were saddled with tougher chores: raking leaves, stacking wood, shoveling snow. School chums who slept over on weekends were handed rakes and shovels and conscripted into the Davis cleanup crew. When Shelby was 8 or so, he and Diana lobbied their father for a swimming pool, pointing out that there was plenty of room for one next to the tennis court (a rare Davis indulgence). Davis gave tentative approval: The family had to agree to dig the hole by hand, to avoid an expensive backhoe rental. The children couldn't believe that Davis was serious about a do-it-yourself excavation measuring 15 by 40 feet with a depth of as much as 8 feet, but they went along with Plan A because there wasn't any Plan B. Kathryn was smart enough to stay indoors while the others picked and shoveled during two exhausting weekends. The results were: a small pile of dirt and several large calluses. On the third weekend, the amateur excavators hit bedrock. As Shelby and Diana struggled to contain their glee, their father called off the dig. He hired bulldozers to finish the job.

On paper, Shelby was his father's clone. Like Davis, he'd prepped at Lawrenceville and attended Princeton. He majored in history, not accounting, and chose not to pursue an MBA. He worked in his father's office on breaks from school. He wrote for the college daily (his father had been an editor of the same paper, the *Princetonian*). He helped produce the "Careers in Insurance" supplement, which involved selling ads to his father's business contacts and writing about the various facets of the industry. He interviewed Russian scholars (his father's friends) for an article on Soviet politics (his father's academic specialty) that was published in the *New York Times*. He considered pursuing an insurance career (his father's investment specialty) but he already fancied a career on Wall Street (his father's bailiwick).

Shelby met his wife-to-be during a summer tour of Europe after he had completed his junior year at Princeton. His best friend in college, Keith Kroeger, picked the cities, and the two Princetonians met up with two Vassarians in Rome. Shelby had girlfriends back home—his mother preferred one named Pamela. But when in Rome, he fell for Wendy Adams. Again, he followed in his father's footsteps; Davis, too, had found his future bride during a trip to Europe. Kathryn came from a wealthy Philadelphia family; Wendy from a wealthy Boston family. During Wendy's first visit to the Davis summer house in Maine, Shelby took her on an easy climb up a local mountain. She passed a Davis test for prospective brides: Were they as pleasant at the end of the climb as they had been at the outset? Shelby proposed. He was 21; Wendy was 20. They married the next summer, after graduation. The marriage lasted 17 years.

During Shelby's senior year at Princeton, his father hinted at a job offer. Shelby ignored the overture. He wanted to work on Wall Street but preferred to be a stock analyst. Having heard Davis compliment the research department at The Bank of New York, he signed up for an interview with one of the bank's recruiters. The recruiters promised him a chance to start researching companies right away, without having to waste time at a teller's window or interning in the appraisal or loan departments. Shelby was enthralled. The bank hired him forthwith, at $87 a week.

Shelby and Wendy moved into a Manhattan apartment. He and his new father-in-law, Weston Adams, quickly developed mutual admiration. Adams was a successful financier who had served as president of the Boston Stock Exchange and also founded a well-known investment house: Adams, Harkness, and Hill. He was also a sports-loving bon vivant whose family had owned the Suffolk Downs Racetrack. His purchase of the Boston Bruins brought Canadian-style hockey to America. Shelby impressed him with his work ethic, modesty, and business savvy. He chose Shelby as treasurer of the Bruins. He took Shelby along on the occasional scouting trip, looking for young hockey talent. On weekends, they watched games together in the family box.

Shelby's first boss, Peter LeBay, was an amiable number cruncher. LeBay didn't ask Shelby to cover the industry Shelby knew best, because, in spite of the fantastic run-up in stock prices, insurance was considered a marginal and sleepy prospect. Instead, Shelby was assigned to the heavyweights of U.S. industry: companies with staying power and economic clout; companies that would have been voted most likely to succeed in the future. "Just like being in college," Shelby said, referring to the stack of term papers he produced on the makers and sellers of steel, rubber, aluminum, oil, copper, and cement.

Each term paper included charts and tables, so the reader could compare profit margins, earnings, sales, and so on, going back several years. "You'd notice if a company had lowered its costs, raised its profits, and accelerated its growth," Shelby says. "If a company performed better than its peers, you'd see why. Once you had this data, it was easy to question management about the company's future. Would a favorable trend continue? What were they doing to make things happen?"

Lingering at the bank after hours, Shelby thumbed through financial magazines, newsletters, and reports by other analysts, looking for unusual angles. The generic viewpoint didn't interest him, and crunching numbers didn't satisfy him. He realized he couldn't judge a company's prospects by sitting at a desk with a slide rule and an adding machine (calculators weren't readily available). Soon after his arrival, he lobbied his boss to let him make corporate house calls, where he could meet managers and quiz them in person, the way his father had. Most analysts didn't stray far from their desks, and few actually visited companies on their research lists. With no chance to rate the leadership, how could they separate doers from bluffers? The bank wasn't wild about Shelby's plan to turn analysis into investigative reporting, but he got a tentative go-ahead and a modest travel budget.

Investor relations departments didn't exist yet, and companies were as unprepared for Shelby's visits as his bank was unsure of the benefits of sending him. At age 22, Shelby found himself sitting in executive suites, talking directly to CEOs his father's age.

In his role as tire-and-rubber analyst, he flew to Akron, Ohio—the Detroit of the tread trade—to meet with the industry's Big Five (Goodyear, Firestone, General Tire, Cooper, and UniRoyal). These competitors were headquartered within a 10-mile radius, and Shelby saw them all during one trip in 1959. The tire business was cyclical; its profits rose and fell with the economy, and tire stocks rose and fell accordingly. The gyrations of cyclicals contributed to the widespread conviction that stocks were untrustworthy.

The midpoint of the bull run that carried Davis's net worth into eight figures was 1959, but it hadn't attracted Main Street buyers. The public, by and large, still owned the "prudent" investment: bonds, but the sorry performance of bonds mocked their prudence. Bond investments continued to disappoint; stock investments were pleasant surprises. Stocks had been the losing assets at the zenith of their popularity in the late 1920s; they became unpopular winning assets in the 1950s.

The Dow was dominated by the big shots of heavy industry on Shelby's research list—rubber, autos, cement, aluminum. (Most are much smaller shots today.) Companies in these industries were touted as high-quality, low-risk, and good for the long haul in any portfolio. Already, the Reynolds Metals and Alcoas had begun to falter, but even the most pessimistic analysts didn't foresee the abandoned refineries and shuttered factories left to rust, or how gritty industry would never recover its profitability and would disappoint investors for the rest of the century.

Fast-food restaurants, shopping malls, and chain stores would soon spread from coast to coast, but who knew then that McDonald's, Dunkin' Donuts, and Kentucky Fried Chicken would someday become more valuable and more rewarding to shareholders than almighty U.S. Steel?

Shelby quickly advanced through the cubicles and became head of equity research at The Bank of New York. At age 25, he was named a vice president—the youngest since Alexander Hamilton. After his promotion, he was told he had a shot at bank president if he stuck around for 30 years. That prospect became less and less appealing the more he thought about it. "I saw myself attending one formal dinner after another. Basically stuck in a glorified public relations job. I realized I'd rather review 100 financial statements and quiz 100 CEOs than host a cocktail party with the bank's preferred 100 clients."

Shelby made many good research calls and a few bad ones. When asked about the latter, he replied: "Analysts always remember their mistakes and try to learn from them."

He never forgot Reynolds Aluminum. Forty years after the act, Shelby still wishes he hadn't recommended it in a 1960 report. Reynolds was one of aluminum's "Big Four," along with Alcoa, Alcan, and Kaiser. This foursome dominated the world market. Alcoa enjoyed a monopolistic lock on production before World War II, but, to create competitors for Alcoa, the government built aluminum plants and sold them to Reynolds and Kaiser. To increase the odds of survival, the government gave the two new companies zero-interest loans to pay for the plants. "Certificates of necessity," the loans were called. Meanwhile, an antitrust action forced Alcoa to spin off its Canadian subsidiary, Alcan, creating the third rival.

Aluminum was in high demand, so there was plenty of business for all four companies. They worked overtime to handle the orders during the Korean War.

In his May 1960 "Survey of the Aluminum Industry," Shelby noted that aluminum companies were expensive to operate and, after a vigorous run-up in the 1950s, their stocks had gotten expensive (25 to 40 times earnings). Yet he ignored these defects and gave a buy signal based on aluminum's bright future. He put it in Wall Streetese: "Current high stock market valuations of present earnings are justifiable on a long-term basis."

His favorite was Reynolds, selling below its 1956 all-time-high price. A visit to the Reynolds headquarters in Richmond, Virginia, got him excited. He and his fellow analysts were routed through a giant hangar where full-scale models of products "soon to be made from aluminum" were displayed from floor to ceiling. Everything from cars to furniture, locomotives to bridges, could be sculpted from this lightweight metal, and it promised huge potential sales to the aircraft manufacturers.

Back in the office, Shelby wrote a rave review and recommended Reynolds at 40 times earnings. He fancied that it could double its earnings every three years, thereby turning an expensive proposition into a screaming bargain. A terrific growth stock, he thought. After all, Reynolds had been growing fast ever since it was launched.

This was one case, in which visiting a company and chatting with management led Shelby astray. While he was in Richmond marveling at what he'd seen in the hangar, unsold aluminum was piling up in company warehouses. Analysts were unaware of this backlog because the warehouses weren't part of the tour.

In spite of the exciting new uses for aluminum, the supply had far outdistanced the demand. Prices fell, profits collapsed, and the stocks took a bungee. Four decades later, Reynolds and other metals stocks are selling for less than they did when Eisenhower was president and Johnny Mathis was a teen idol. Shelby had witnessed the peril of buying high-priced growth. He'd also learned that typical corporate managers emphasize the positive and, if they can get away with it, neglect to mention the negatives.

Davis tended his insurance portfolio from his office at 110 William Street. Once in a while, his son dropped in for some perfunctory shop talk, but Davis had no interest in aluminum, rubber, auto, or concrete companies. Manufacturers such as these required expensive factories, and repairs and upgrades depleted their cash. They tended to lose money in recessions, so their earnings were unreliable. They were always vulnerable to some new process or invention that could put them out of business. The entire history of manufacturing had produced few long-term survivors, and only companies that had reinvented themselves had escaped obsolescence. Several insurance companies had celebrated their 200th birthdays, and were still selling essentially the same product they sold when the Founding Fathers were alive. They profited from investing their customers' money; manufacturers never got that chance. Shelby didn't follow the insurance industry, but his stint at The Bank of New York had taught him that banks had a lot in common with his father's favorite sector. Banks and insurers tended to operate out of marble, filigreed headquarters that resembled jumbo mausoleums. Banking never went out of style because money never went out of style. Shelby's own employer was proof of this. The Bank of New York had been founded in the eighteenth century.

Along with its longevity, banking had developed a stodgy reputation. Because banks were never trendy, investors were never inclined to pay scalpers' premiums to own them. Ergo, you could always buy bank shares at bargain rates relative to other types of shares and invest in a bank's growth on the cheap.

A bank profited from other people's money, but only if that money was prudently deployed. Reckless lending was an occupational hazard, but the risks were minimized by skilled managers who did not let their greed strangle their caution.

It would take more than a decade for Shelby to fill his mutual fund portfolio with banks and other financials, but The Bank of New York gave him an insider's familiarity with the group.

CHAPTER 6

COOL TRIO RUNS HOT FUND

SHELBY'S ESCAPE FROM THE BANK OF NEW York was hatched at a Christmas party in 1965. Having downed a few eggnogs, he and Guy Palmer, a Yale grad and a fellow bank vice president, decided to open their own freelance investment firm. Once again, Shelby had flattered his father by imitation. He abandoned a paying job in favor of insecure self-employment. Davis had done the same 20 years earlier.

The two escapees tried to recruit Jeremy Biggs, a portfolio manager at the $1 billion U.S. Steel pension fund, as a third partner. They'd met Biggs through his father, a much-admired executive at the bank Shelby and Palmer had left behind, and a helpful ally to Shelby. Biggs saw no point in quitting U.S. Steel to join a rookie enterprise. "You're crazy," he told Shelby. "You don't have any accounts."

After opening a small office, hiring three employees, and attracting a few accounts, Shelby approached Biggs with a second offer. In 1968, Biggs accepted, jilting U.S. Steel. His banker father was skeptical; his mother was supportive. "Nobody in the family ever had his name on a business before," she enthused, referring to the Davis, Palmer and Biggs moniker. Neither Biggs's father nor Shelby's gave their sons any money to manage.

These three musketeers of finance were all in their early thirties. Shelby was short and spare; Palmer, short and chunky; Biggs, tall and lanky. Palmer was the organizer and front man, a prodigious eater and a good talker. He and Biggs enjoyed schmoozing clients; Shelby hated schmoozing. Biggs and Shelby handled most of the stock picking, and both worked overtime, especially in the March rush when companies released their annual reports. But where Biggs was reasonably devoted (he chose dinner with his family over staying late at the office), Shelby was fanatical (he chose the office).

Shelby quizzed as many analysts, investor relations officers, and CEOs as he could cram into a 16-hour schedule. When he wasn't asking questions, he was reading reports to prepare more questions. If he didn't gather every fact, challenge every statement, and, pursue every angle, he felt like a slacker.

In their third year, the trio moved to roomier midtown offices, where they tore down walls to "facilitate communication." At this point, they were handling $100 million in clients' money—some invested in stocks, some in bonds, depending on the client. Shelby put his father on the advisory board for window dressing, but the musketeers later dropped the board altogether. Trophy boards, they realized, didn't win clients. Performance did.

They advertised their services in an old-fashioned brochure with sepia photographs and print that looked like handwriting. This gave the impression of tradition, folksiness, and prudence. In the text, they reversed the image, describing themselves as "imaginative," "objective," and "aggressive."

"Since each account represents different financial circumstances," they wrote, covering all the bases, "we view each client separately and tailor-make investment decisions to coincide with the particular situation. However, no matter how divergent the client's needs may be, one of the primary objectives for our clients is maximum long-term capital appreciation commensurate with reasonable safety."

The mission statement, called "Basic Investment Philosophy," owed a lot to Davis, and though the main points sound obvious today, they were far from obvious to the U.S. investing public in the mid-1960s:

- Stock prices ride on a company's earnings. Eventually, earnings, or the lack of same, determine whether the shareholder wins or loses.
- Earnings ride on the U.S. economy. The reason to be bullish on stocks is that the U.S. economy has a habit of doubling in size every 16 to 18 years, going back more than a century.
- If history repeats itself, the economy will expand eightfold during the adult life of an average investor. Thus, at minimum, an investor can expect a portfolio to generate at least an eightfold gain during his stock-picking career. In periods when stock prices rise faster than earnings, he'll possibly do better. Meanwhile, he'll also benefit from dividends.

This was bedrock logic for steady compounding, and understanding and believing it was all the education required for successful investing. You could win the game with a sensible, diversified portfolio of stocks or mutual funds, and the critical ingredient, time. You didn't need luck, hot tips, or knowing somebody who knew somebody. You didn't need to dodge bears by switching in and out of your holdings. If you thought successful investing depended on luck, hot tips, knowing somebody, or nimble switching, you were a cinch to lose money. Chronic losers often misunderstood the cause of their losses. They thought they were jinxed. Without a solid grounding in the bedrock logic of compounding, it was hard to invest sensibly.

The sepia brochure tells us how Shelby went about picking stocks in this early phase of his career. He was attracted to companies "whose earnings and/or price-earnings ratios are likely to show above-average expansion," which sounded a lot like the Davis Double Play. But the fact that he didn't put a limit on how much he'd pay for earnings was a departure from Davis. Shelby watched for "industries that are changing their characteristics," and he kept track of "the shifting of investor interest among various industries" just as he'd done as an analyst. He and Biggs didn't specialize in certain types of companies, and they showed no particular interest in insurance or banking. They readily revamped their clients' portfolios to take advantage of trends. Davis never cared about trends, but in the go-go era of the late 1960s, trendy high-tech stocks ruled the market. Investing in high-tech soon gave the musketeers their comeuppance.

Shelby and Biggs began managing New York Venture Fund in February 1969. America was bogged down in Vietnam, inflation was on the rise, and the almighty dollar was losing both its buying power and the respect of the rest of the world. Stocks had rallied after a short bear market back in 1966, but another decline was in progress. Taking charge of a fledgling fund near the latest bear bottom was lucky timing—at least temporarily. New investors supplied the New York Venture Fund with $2 million in fresh cash—a pittance for most mutual funds, but enough to double New York Venture Fund's assets. Shelby and Biggs put their cash to work buying depressed shares, while most of their competitors had no cash on hand.

It was hard to see the Davis influence in these initial maneuvers. Shelby and Biggs bought an array of small, fast-growing companies—everything from McDonald's and Dunkin' Donuts to nursing home franchises, medical suppliers, real estate developers, and a couple of oil refiners. Shelby bought four of his father's favorite insurance names, including AIG and GEICO, but less than 10 percent of the portfolio was riding on insurance and financials. Fannie Mae, the dominant player in the mortgage business, was already in the fund when Shelby and Biggs took over, and they promptly sold it. More than a decade later, Shelby bought it back, and Fannie became one of his most rewarding ideas.

Their biggest positions were high-tech. With Palmer out trolling for clients, Shelby and Biggs decked the portfolio with Memorex, Digital Equipment, American Micro Systems, and Mohawk Data. "Data" and "systems" were the buzzwords that attracted investors to the technology hive, where prices were steep and expectations buoyant, in spite of the latest market setback. Financial pundits declared this a New Era of American Ingenuity, repeating a phrase coined by their predecessors in the late 1920s. Shelby was attracted to the "high earnings visibility" of the New Era companies. To be successful, a writer must find a voice and an investor must find a style. In his impatience to prove himself, Shelby lost sight of his father's maxims and was carried away by the go-go drumbeat. It was hard not to do otherwise.

The results from the first year were indeed extraordinary, just as Shelby had suggested in the interview with *Institutional Investor*. While 144 competitors had reported a loss, New York Venture was up 25.3 percent. Of his rookie success, Shelby said, "We all thought we were geniuses." "Cool Trio Runs Hot Fund," gushed *Business Week* in a congratulatory piece that appeared on February 7, 1970. In the photo that ran with the article, Shelby has sideburns and looks very mod. Biggs and Shelby denied they were go-go investors, or "gunslingers," although Memorex and several other tech picks were clearly go-go stocks. "Buy a good company," Biggs said, defending their strategy, "and even if it's overpriced, you know it's a good company."

Shelby elaborated. "We guarantee that we will never be number one in a roaring speculative bull market. We eschew the go-go philosophy that last year made instant winners of funds that favored new issues and hotshot over-the-counter securities." Yet their holdings were considerably more hotshot than Davis would have tolerated.

By March 1970, the Cool Trio had attracted $55 million in new capital. As soon as the capital arrived, and with the *Business Week* plaudits fresh in investors' minds, Memorex dropped 20 percent in a single day on a bad earnings report. Shelby and Biggs bought more. Halfway through Memorex's swoon from $168 to $3, they bought again. They bailed out at $20, taking a big loss.

Memorex was a fast grower with a fancy price tag—a fatal combination when the profits disappear and investors fall out of love. Then, the Davis Double Play goes into reverse. Let's say a beloved faster grower sells at 30 times earnings and earns $1 a share, creating a $30 stock. If the earnings drop by half and disenchanted investors decide to pay only 15 times earnings, the $30 stock suddenly becomes a $7.50 stock. When further disenchantment drops the price to 10 times earnings, a $30 investment is whittled to $5. The "Cool Trio Runs Hot Fund" article marked the end of the hot streak.

"Memorex wounded us all," said Biggs, but it wasn't the only high-tech flop in the portfolio. Computer Tape was another. The New York Venture Fund went from champ to chump. The number-one fund in its rookie year landed in the bottom 10 percent in the year that followed. The math was discouraging.

To devote his full attention to bringing the New York Venture Fund out of its tailspin, Shelby declined an invitation from Bill Wasserman to join the board of the Wasserman family trusts in Philadelphia. With his usual edgy humor, Bill had cracked, "We could use some more of your half-baked ideas." Shelby couldn't entirely disagree. His confidence was shaken, and more shakes were to come. "My father had five years of glory at the outset of his investing," Shelby recalls. "I was about to experience five years of hell at the outset of mine.

The sharp decline of 1969 to 1970 had been quickly forgotten.

Buyers returned to stocks with gusto, but they'd lost their affection for the washed-out tech variety. The money tide had shifted; it flowed out of the go-gos and into larger, safer, wondrous blue chips that comprised the so-called Nifty Fifty. These were established brand names: Avon, Polaroid, Gillette, Coca-Cola, IBM, Xerox, McDonald's, and others. During the first half of the twentieth century, the economy lurched from boom to bust, and people didn't expect companies to provide steady, consistent profit growth. Starting in the 1940s, the busts were less busty, and owning growth companies became fashionable. By the early 1970s, it had become wildly fashionable. At their priciest, many Nifties sold for 40 to 50 and a few higher than 70 times earnings, but the Street's analysts pronounced these "one-decision stocks" worth owning at any price. They were applauded by analysts, who touted the group as fast growers for the long haul, and much less risky than the fly-by-nights in the computer arena. Buy them, forget them, and in a few years, whatever you paid, you'll be glad you paid it.

Original Nifty Fifty[a]

Company	Stock Price[b]	P/E Ratio
Polaroid	$ 63	97
Simplicity Pattern	54	50
Disney	6.50	82
Avon Products	68	63
ITT	60	16
Schlitz Brewing	58	37
Xerox	50	47
Hueblein, Inc.	58	31
Coca-Cola	3	44
McDonald's	3.75	75
JCPenney	22.50	31
Gillette	4	25
American Express	16	38
Sears	58	29
Chesebrough-Ponds	44	40
Eastman Kodak	66	44
Anheuser-Busch	4.50	33
Kmart Corp.	16	49
General Electric	9	25
PepsiCo	1.60	27
IBM	80	36
American Hospital Supply	33	50
3M	21	40
Squibb	26	34
Louisiana Land and Exploration	48	25
Digital Equipment	15	61
AMP Inc.	7	47
Emery Air Freight	30	55
International Flavors and Fragrances	14	72
Black & Decker	36	51
Baxter International	14	73
Johnson & Johnson	5.40	60
Revlon	36	25
Burroughs	37	46
Bristol-Myers	4.30	27
Procter & Gamble	14	33
Citicorp	19	21
Texas Instruments	15	42

Original Nifty Fifty[a] (Continued)

Company	Stock Price[b]	P/E Ratio
Merck	5	45
Schering-Plough	8.50	48
Pfizer	5	28
Upjohn	7	41
Philip Morris	4	25
American Home Products	10	38
Eli Lilly	10	43
Lubrizol	11	34
Halliburton	23	37
Dow Chemical	17	25
Schlumberger	12	46
MGIC Investment	N/A	
Average P/E	$42.7	

Source: Montgomery Securities.
[a] As of December 31, 1972.
[b] Rounded to nearest whole number.

1938   Shelby Davis, age one.

Early 1940s   Shelby with sister, Diana, outside Tarrytown Homestead.

1947 Shelby Cullom Davis, now with his own firm, becomes president of the New York Society of Security Analysts.

Mid-1950s Kathryn W. Davis photographed for her 25th wedding anniversary.

1972 Ambassador and Mrs. Shelby Cullom Davis returning to Switzerland from a trip to the Soviet Union.

1970s Shelby Cullom Davis appearing in white tie at a Mayflower Society function.

1993 The two Shelbys, father and son, near the family retreat in Maine.

1995 Shelby and sons, Chris and Andrew, meet in New Mexico to discuss transfer of Davis operations to the third generation.

1995 Chris, Andrew, and Shelby (after a bike accident) at Davis Investment Seminar.

1996 Chris and Shelby being photographed for a *Forbes* article.

1993 Chris and Andrew outside Chris's Fifth Avenue office soon after both became Davis fund managers.

CHAPTER 7

DAVIS AND SHELBY COMPOUND

DAVIS HAD RETURNED TO AMERICA IN 1975 with Kathryn in tow. They landed in Hartford and headed for the nearest soda fountain—what they'd missed most in six years in Switzerland was milkshakes. The Tarrytown house, Davis's investment firm, and his portfolio all had seen better days. The house suffered a fire and a succession of careless tenants; the firm, such as it was, suffered a reduction in commission revenue that followed the SEC's Mayday edict; the portfolio suffered the twin bear markets of 1969 to 1970 and 1973 to 1974.

When he arrived in Switzerland in 1969, the ambassador's net worth hovered around $50 million. Six years later, he returned to the United States $30 million poorer. His stocks had failed him, as they had failed everybody in the bear market of 1973 to 1974. The caretaker of his portfolio, Ken Ebbitt, had presided over the wreckage in his absence, but Davis didn't blame his stand-in for the market's mischief. Even if Ebbitt had advised Davis to sell, it's unlikely his boss would have listened.

Absorbed in his ambassadorship, a night of jet lag away from Wall Street, Davis was spared the remorse and second-guessing of active investors who'd kept track of their plummeting net worth in the daily stock tables or on their Quotrons. Insurance didn't hold up well in this pecuniary quicksand. In fact, many insurers were mired deeper than the typical manufacturer in the S&P index. Property-casualty dropped from $150 to $60. Life and health insurers went down from $280 to $120 before Wall Street found a bottom. These declines were typical for the period.

Davis had correctly predicted hard times for auto and casualty at the start of the decade. "Insurance is in a down cycle," he'd told Shelby. Yet, given Davis's appetite for margin, his 60 percent loss (from $50 million to $20 million) was well contained. Without Japan and without changing the mix in his portfolio, 1973 to 1974 might have wiped him out.

He held onto the life insurers and the Japanese holdings that were his biggest winners in the bull market, but he jettisoned some of his U.S. casualty and auto insurers. He upped his stake in AIG, the global insurance conglomerate he'd discovered in Japan. The company was multifaceted, creative, international, and parsimonious, just like its autocratic CEO, Hank Greenberg, who lived on a fraction of his wherewithal. Davis's AIG stake had already increased through AIG acquisitions. Every time Greenberg bought a mom-and-pop insurer Davis already owned, Davis got more AIG stock.

Davis's losses did not put a slump in Davis's work habits. He attacked his job with his usual gusto, arriving early and leaving late with his briefcase crammed with reports.

Why shouldn't Davis be enthusiastic? Stocks were cheap in 1976. Didn't Warren Buffett say he felt like an oversexed teenager at a dance hall? Bargains were as prevalent as when Davis began to invest a generation earlier. In June 1975, he wrote a special report to his newsletter subscribers, in case somebody bothered to read it: "The biggest improvement in fire-casualty earnings since the end of inflation after World War II lies ahead . . . interest in fire-casualty issues could well rekindle interest in life insurance stocks."

Davis's financial life had three phases: learn, earn, and return. The learn phase lasted into his early forties, and the earn phase stretched from his forties into his late seventies. At that point, he tackled the return phase, turning his attention to the lucky would-be recipients of the money he'd hoarded and tended so devotedly. Earlier, he'd made the donation to Princeton ($5.3 million for the history chair) and established professorships at Wellesley, Trinity College, and the Fletcher School of Diplomacy at Tufts. His generosity built and filled libraries at Lincoln Center, Bradley University, and New York's College of Insurance. Some of these bequests remained in his control so he (and, later, his grandson Chris) could handle the investing. He wasn't inclined to bestow more gifts on academia, and he continued to oppose any large giveaways to his family. Davis reiterated to Chris what he'd said decades earlier to Shelby and Diana: "You're getting nothing from me. That way, you won't be robbed of the pleasure of earning it yourself."

Davis's insurance portfolio added $500 million to his net worth in the 1980s. Davis's fortune had totally eclipsed the once-considerable Wasserman fortune, most of which was tied up in family trusts that were constantly losing ground to his portfolio. What pluck, luck, genius, talent, enterprise (and in some cases, con artistry) create in one generation, dependency, cash drain, and Uncle Sam destroy in the next two. Not in Davis's case, but if his offspring weren't entitled to his spoils, and schools weren't getting them, who was?

Warren Buffett intended to shunt his billions into zero population growth, to help save the planet from the glut of humans, even though fewer humans meant fewer consumers to buy products from his favorite multinationals: Coke, Gillette, and AIG insurance.

When Davis turned 74, he prepared his exit strategy in a similar fashion naming his favorite causes, though zero population wasn't the designated beneficiary. On a flight from Europe, in September 1983, he clarified his intentions in a memo: "I am writing these lines on TWA's London–New York flight 703 economy," he began, after explaining he was sitting in coach. "Always a believer in waste not, want not, I have set aside this time to endeavor to answer the question." The question, basically, was: Who gets the money? The answer was: Conservative causes. Whereas Buffett opted to invest his lump in a less crowded planet, Davis preferred to support the furtherance of the capitalism and free enterprise that had allowed him to amass his lump. In his view, higher taxes, bigger government, and socialist ideologues threatened financial bounty.

In a multipage "final note," Davis asked himself why he hadn't provided "castles and plantations for the children and super-jets for the grandchildren." He answered as follows:

> Where is the incentive if children and grandchildren start out with a trust fund which guarantees they never had to work? [He refused to condemn his offspring to a "life of ease" because] from my own experience and that of trust fund friends, I know such hapless (not lucky) recipients often if not usually become the victims of society, in the care of psychologists, psychiatrists and others. I believe in providing a "safety net" in case of emergency but, predominantly, I believe in the incentive to excel . . . and contribute to the common good.

He stuck this memo in a drawer at the office. His family never saw it, but the contents wouldn't have surprised them. Nobody in the Davis clan expected to inherit the Davis reward.

Shelby had lived and worked independently of Davis. His father's financial scorecard only interested him as a point of reference against which he could measure New York Venture Fund's performance. Otherwise, he continued to keep his professional distance. His mutual funds didn't yet carry the Davis moniker. He worked out of Fiduciary Trust, a long cab ride from his father's office. His business card read "consultant" and provided no further details. His goal was to try to continue as the best-performing anonymous money manager on Wall Street.

In a 1979 speech, "The '80s Are Coming," Shelby had foreseen the end to Mr. Market's doldrums. In spite of the pesky inflation, Shelby said, "The news could get amazingly good." Stocks were priced for amazingly bad news, and many companies were selling for less than their book value and at single-digit multiples.

On the economic front, the Fed's traditional inflation-killing tactic—raising short-term interest rates—had failed to produce the desired result, but cigar-chomping Fed chairman Paul Volcker led the fight into the 1980s with Churchillian aplomb. Volcker kept up the raises and strangled the money supply until the government's prime lending rate soared to 20½ percent and 30-year Treasuries paid investors 15 percent to own them. A 15 percent coupon attached to Uncle Sam's IOU was the bond deal of the century—the riskier stock market returned only 10 to 11 percent over time. Yet mainstream investors shunned this glorious bond windfall just as eagerly as they had embraced 2.5 percent Treasuries—the sucker play of the century—a generation earlier.

Eventually, the financial law of gravity asserted itself. What went up for 34 years, came down. A sure sign of inflation's imminent demise was the gold and silver frenzy of 1980, when popular demand sent the gold price to $700-plus and the silver tab to $40-plus. Across the country, people scrapped their silverware, watches, chains, and trophies for the metal's value. Expert gold bugs predicted $1,000 gold and $100 silver, but prices quickly went south and never turned north.

The New York Venture Fund had its best year to date in 1980: up 31.9 percent, nearly doubling the gains in the S&P 500 and tripling the gains in the Dow. The fund passed a milestone—it was up more than 100 percent since its starting date 11 years earlier, while the S&P 500 was up only 18.8 percent and the Dow was down 0.3 percent! With dividends reinvested, an initial $10,000 put into the New York Venture Fund was now worth $23,524.

As the inflationary swell receded, bondholders and stockholders were about to enjoy a 20-year fall in interest rates. But before stocks responded, they gave investors one last bear scare that kicked off what would prove to be the greatest bull market of the century. In 1981, the economy fell into recession and the Dow declined 24 percent. Sizable declines in companies involved in farm equipment (Harvester), metals (Inco), and asbestos (Manville) gave more hints that the hard-asset prosperity was over.

The signal for a momentous turnaround came when the Fed dropped rates. Shelby realized Volcker's anti-inflation crusade had succeeded in changing the Big Picture. In 1947, Davis had foreseen a prolonged period of rising rates. In 1981, Shelby foresaw the reverse. He began to specialize—cutting back on New York Venture's eclectic holdings and concentrating on fewer industries. He sold his oil and gas positions, figuring the gritty industries had had their run and would struggle as inflation abated.

The Reagan years added $1 trillion of debt to the federal balance sheet, equaling the prior IOU from the entire history of the U.S. Government. Consumers and companies alike followed Washington's lead. The entire nation had put itself in hock to the tune of $8 trillion by the late 1980s, up from $1.2 trillion in 1970.

With rates in reverse, the idea was to borrow as much as possible and buy whatever you could with it, including golf courses, major corporations, and high-priced art. The Pebble Beach golf course in California went for a hefty premium: $900 million. Van Gogh's *Irises* was auctioned at Sotheby's for $53.9 million, just before the 1987 Crash. Oil heiress Joan Payson Whitney had paid $84,000 for the painting in 1947, the year Davis started collecting insurance shares. The *Irises* price tag amazed the world, but the compounded return on this canvas was far less than Davis's return on stock certificates. His net worth had reached $386 million in 1987. That same year, one of Davis's Japanese holdings, Yasuda Fire and Marine, paid $39 million for Van Gogh's *Sunflowers,* a useless expenditure in Davis's view. That money could have been invested in Japanese stocks or bonds for further compounding, but the Japanese were bent on conspicuous consumption. They bought Rockefeller Center as well as Pebble Beach. Soon, they wouldn't be able to afford either one.

This was the heyday of the leveraged buyout, when Mike Milken and his junk-bond groupies held their famous gathering, the Predator's Ball. With access to Milken's magical pool of capital, small shots like Nelson Peltz of Triangle Industries captured large American corporations and sold them for parts. This chop-shop strategy held Wall Street in its thrall and led to a wave of so-called "hostile takeovers" that were sometimes overpriced and often ill-advised. Thanks to hell-bent leverage, the two largest department store chains in America became the property of a Canadian loon named Campeau.

Acting on a different theme—that falling rates favored paper assets and not brick, mortar, and baubles—Shelby populated the New York Venture Fund with financial stocks that had underachieved in the hard-asset prosperity of the 1970s. Besides being timely, bank shares were very affordable. They were selling at 10 times earnings, and their earnings were growing at a steady 12 to 15 percent. Banks' stodgy reputation caused investors to underrate their future prospects. This was a perfect setup for the latest Davis Double Play.

Shelby had learned the banking business during his apprenticeship at The Bank of New York. Banks had a lot in common with his father's beloved insurers. A bank didn't manufacture anything, so it didn't need expensive factories, finicky machinery, warehouses, research labs, or high-priced PhDs. It didn't pollute, so it spent zilch on pollution-control devices. It didn't sell gadgets or ready-to-wear, so it could avoid hiring a sales force. It didn't ship merchandise, so it had no shipping costs. Its sole product was money, borrowed from depositors and lent out to borrowers. Money came in different guises (coins, paper, blips on a screen), but was never obsolete. Banks competed with other banks, but banking itself was always in vogue. You couldn't say the same for horse-drawn carriages, oil lamps, passenger trains, telegraph machines, typewriters, gramophones, and a fat Rolodex of prominent industries undone by the next bright idea. An inspired nerd in Palo Alto might invent the next gizmo that puts half of Silicon Valley out of business, but banking lived on.

As mentioned earlier, several banks dated from the era of the Founding Fathers. Among them was The Bank of New York, where Alexander Hamilton was the youngest vice president on record until Shelby came along. Only a handful of manufacturers could match such longevity, and they survived only because their quick thinking CEOs got them out of outmoded activities and into new products.

Like insurance, banking bored most people. Racy novels about bankers were in short supply, although a bond salesman was a main character in *The Great Gatsby*. An exciting run-up in a bank stock was a rare event. Unless they were involved in a merger or a takeover bid, banks rarely made the list of daily big movers in the financial pages. Atlanta had its Coca-Cola millionaires; Bentonville, Arkansas, its Wal-Mart millionaires; and Seattle, Washington, was soon to be populated with Microsoft millionaires. But you didn't hear about clusters of millionaires who got that way by owning Wells Fargo, Chase Manhattan, or First Union.

The risky part of banking was its small margin for error. A bank made money on its depositors' money; it borrowed from Peter to lend to Paul. Normally, a bank had enough capital to cover roughly 5 to 6 percent of its outstanding loans. If more than 5 percent of its loans to the Pauls went sour, it had no way to pay back all the Peters. And if too many Peters withdrew their money at once, the bank was sunk.

In spite of their dark suits and their funeral-parlor demeanor, bankers could, at times, succumb to irrational exuberance and act like day traders. In a buoyant economy, they made loans to questionable projects and less reliable borrowers. Borrowers kept up with their payments in prosperous times, so banks had fewer defaults to contend with. With fewer defaults, they put less money aside to cover potential losses. This raised banks' earnings and generally resulted in higher stock prices.

In a sluggish economy, consumers hoarded cash and a happy chain of events could quickly turn unhappy. Bankers got pickier about lending to the next Paul because earlier Pauls had defaulted on their loans. As losses mounted, banks shored up their reserves with money that otherwise would count as earnings. As problems expanded, earnings contracted.

To escape from such a predicament, banks needed help. Usually, they got it when the Fed cut short-term interest rates. Falling short rates were manna to bankers, especially when long-term rates stayed relatively lofty. In that case, a bank borrowed for less and lent for more, boosting its profit on the wider "spread."

Whenever the economy hit a recessionary pothole, as it did in 1981, investors turned pessimistic and the prognosis for bank stocks was decidedly gloomy. Prices reflected the gloom, and canny buyers were rewarded. Knowing a few bank CEOs came in handy. From the horse's mouth, Shelby got status reports on the health of the rest of the horse. Often, a banker's informed appraisal was more optimistic than analysts' or journalists' appraisals, which already had created bargains. (When a CEO was hard to reach, Shelby sometimes waited and made a follow-up call from a vacation spot. His would-be source would be flattered, thinking that Shelby had interrupted his fun to pick his brain.)

By 1983, Shelby's strategy had combined his favorite banks, and some of his father's favorite insurers (Chubb, Lincoln National), with the strongest companies in other fields, especially computers (IBM, Motorola, Intel) and pharmaceuticals (Merck). He never found his Japan, but his father's success abroad caused him to invest in multinationals. He found appealing prospects in several global financial operators, including AIG and Morgan Stanley.

In the early stages of AIG's remarkable expansion, an earnest perusal of all the available numbers wouldn't have foretold this company's remarkable future as a high-octane compounding machine. It was the intangible quality of Hank Greenberg's leadership that made the difference. Shelby, who invested in Greenberg just as his father had, saw the same managerial knack in a more eclectic lineup of tough-minded, militaristic sticklers who had a distaste for excuses and a devotion to the bottom line.

Thanks to another charismatic boss, Andy Grove, Shelby took a rewarding ride on Intel. In his money management firm, he'd invested in the company before Intel was public. He dumped the shares for a sevenfold profit before the price was cut in half in 1973 to 1974. He'd already been burned by Memorex and other tech wrecks, and a submerging Intel intensified Shelby's aversion to tech stocks in general. Then a friend introduced him to Grove, Intel's new CEO. Here was another straight-talking workaholic who had a talent for one-liners. Shelby wrote down his favorite: "There are two kinds of companies—the quick and the dead." He was able to buy this wondrous enterprise at a single-digit multiple, and Intel has been a fixture in the New York Venture Fund for more than a decade.

With Shelby on top of his game, Wall Street got the biggest boost in two decades: The Dow went up 48 percent; the S&P, up 58 percent, and New York Venture, up 68 percent. In one year, Shelby's fund bagged more profit than in the entire decade since the last bear market. Such surges were unpredictable. To avoid missing them, you had to stay in stocks permanently *and,* you had to reinvest your capital gains and dividends. This was and is a crucial and often overlooked factor in fundholder prosperity. The Fund was typical. If you bought $10,000 worth of the Fund at the outset and pocketed your gains, your investment grew to $17,902 by 1986. If you let the money ride, it grew to $75,074!

Many investors were too bored or too scared to let their money ride. They adopted a quick-in/quick-out strategy that hadn't been popular since Gerald Loeb's best-seller touted the practice in the 1930s. An array of market-timing newsletters met the demand in the 1980s. During the quick *in* phase, the market timers brought a lot of business to their chosen mutual funds, so funds tolerated the alliance. Then the money left just as readily, and managers were forced to keep a cash stash to cover the redemptions that were sapping their overall returns. "The market timing guys drove us crazy early in the decade," Shelby says. "We tolerated them for a while, but soon enough, their poor performance lost them popularity and credibility. We added extra fees to discourage frequent switching."

Bank stocks nearly tripled from 1981 to 1987, and the Dow also dazzled, hurtling past 2000 to reach a record top of 2722 in the summer of 1987. The Japanese Nikkei celebrated its all-time high as well, but from there it was all downhill in Tokyo and on Wall Street. A setback in bonds and a weaker dollar were the usual bearish portents.

This time, the wealth destruction was quick and vicious. By October, the Dow had shed 36 percent, including a panicky one-day drop of 508 points or nearly 23 percent—a bear market in a single trading session and the unkindest one-day loss in history. A sophisticated hedging system called "portfolio insurance" was designed to protect big investment houses from such air pockets, but, instead, the system aggravated the decline. The pundit majority was calling for Dow 3600, and they got Dow 1700 instead. Influential talking heads doubted the survival of the world financial system.

"One question on many people's minds is, 'How long can this outstanding American stock market keep going up?'" wrote Davis, who'd signed the annual letter to the New York Venture Fund shareholders and sent it out a month before the crash. "The bull market has now had a life of approximately five years. But in spite of traditional thinking that says this . . . may end very soon, a number of economic and political factors indicate to us that this stock market could go substantially higher."

In their views about the future ups and downs of their merchandise, fund managers tended to be no more prescient than their clients, and just as susceptible to misjudgment. Had Shelby

91

acted on his firm's market calls as described in New York Venture Fund's literature, he might have avoided a few setbacks, but who could be sure he'd return to stocks in time for the important rallies? He kept his opinions and emotions out of the portfolio, and advised fundholders to do the same.

The fear persisted for months, and at the annual *Barron's* magazine roundtable, published in January 1988, the expert participants were gloomier than usual. "A bear market has started that will probably last several years," said dour Felix Zulauf. "We have had the first down leg."

"The questions to me," chimed in Paul Tudor Jones, "are not so much . . . will we have a bear market, but will we be able to avert a worldwide depression like we saw in the 1930s?"

"Most stock markets around the world," echoed TV commentator and motorcycle buff Jim Rogers, "are going to go up dramatically . . . but no longer than six months, at which point we are going to have a real bear market. I am talking about a bear market that is just going to wipe out most people in the financial community, most investors around the world. And in fact there are many markets I would short but which I will not be short, because I think they will probably close them down."

As it turned out, there was no worldwide depression and no multiyear bear market. The market stayed open, stock prices rose, and loyal investors were rewarded. The New York Venture Fund had lagged the S&P 500 going into the crash, then lost far less than the index during the crash. Few of Shelby's investors had panicked and sold, so he wasn't forced to ditch future winners to raise cash.

At Davis headquarters, the crash was a thrilling opportunity for Shelby's father. He'd always said a bear market helps you make money, and this was a wondrous example. With TV commentators pondering whether 1987 was 1929 all over again, Davis went on an acquisitive romp. His office manager,

Arnie Widlitz, tried to restrain the boss by hanging up the phone while Davis placed his orders to the trading desk, but Davis grabbed the receiver and dialed again. Several times, Widlitz ended the call, and several times, Davis redialed. "Mr. Davis, you must stop," pleaded Widlitz, who believed his boss was tossing his bankroll at an undertow. "I'm not stopping," groused Davis. "Keep away from that phone."

After the market closed on that infamous "Black Monday," Widlitz had the unpleasant task of telling the boss he'd lost $125 million. The news didn't shake him. "Losing $125 million in the market he could tolerate," said Widlitz, "because a pile of bargains had landed in his lap. Losing $125 out of his wallet would have driven him crazy."

In a post-Crash inspection, the New York Stock Exchange checked the solvency of its member firms, and Davis passed the test, as usual. Though his firm was one of the smallest, according to the Weiss rating agency, it was always one of the strongest. The market value of Davis's assets (the stocks in his portfolio) was 1.5 times greater than his actual capital, reflecting the fact that Davis invested on margin. Merrill Lynch, to compare a pumpkin to a peanut, controlled assets with a market value 20 times greater than its own capital. Large investment houses typically operated much closer to oblivion than Davis did.

Davis made the *Forbes* 400 list of richest Americans on November 14, 1988. *Forbes* pegged the old man's net worth at $370 million (a lowball estimate) and mentioned he'd been named head of the Heritage Foundation. Shelby quipped: "My father's in *Forbes,* unfortunately," meaning this sort of attention was more embarrassing than flattering. That same year, Shelby made the *Forbes* Honor Roll for exceptional fund handling in good markets and bad. His decade-long stretch of 19 percent returns beat mediocrity (the S&P 500) by 4 percent a year and put Shelby within breathing distance of Peter Lynch.

His performance was threatening his anonymity. "My father's certainly done far better than I have," conceded Shelby, then 51.

One of Shelby's best picks in this period was Fannie Mae, formally known as the Federal National Mortgage Association. In the savings and loan (S&L) debacle of the late 1980s, he looked for an investment angle. In his "Crisis Creates Opportunity" mode, he found an obvious beneficiary in Fannie Mae, a buyer and processor of home mortgages.

In cities and towns across America, the same buccaneer spirit that inspired corporate raiders bankrupted hundreds of local thrifts. The S&L wheeler-dealers lacked a Michael Milken to supply other people's money, but they raised it themselves by selling certificates of deposit at irresistible interest rates. CD buyers didn't fret about the solvency of their investment because Uncle Sam guaranteed it. Meanwhile, the CD sellers diverted the proceeds to borrowers for high-risk and grandiose ventures such as Versailles-style hotels and glossy condos. Price was no object, and the recipients of the construction loans often turned out to be related to the lenders. With their solvency in jeopardy, the S&Ls unloaded their mortgage portfolios to raise cash. Fannie Mae, the biggest customer, kept mortgages for the interest payments, or packaged them and sold them for a profit. Either way, Fannie Mae prospered.

The decade of the 1980s was also propitious for insurance stocks. The property-casualty index, which had dropped from 150 to 60 in 1974, jumped all the way to 400. The life and health index rose off its 140 bottom to touch 1,000. These were heady moves. Profit margins were chronically low, as usual. In some years, there was no profit in the industry as a whole.

By all accounts, investment capital planted in this sorry industry had produced a meager harvest. Overhead was high, growth slow, morale low, return on equity sub par, imagination lacking. David Schiff, editor of a sassy and informative newsletter *(Schiff's Insurance Observer*–formerly *Emerson, Reid's Insurance Observer)* echoed Buffett's assessment: "Our industry is populated by an assortment of buffoons, jobbernowls, and chuckleheads. . . . The graduates of top business schools wouldn't be caught dead in the insurance business, and who can blame them? It has negative prestige, the pay is low, and the job security isn't good anymore. Walk into any of the plush new cigar 'clubs' in Manhattan and you'll see a slew of folks who don't work in the insurance business."

Yet if you picked the right stocks, insurance could be highly rewarding. In fact, big money was often made in sluggish industries, as Buffett, Davis, and Peter Lynch had proved. Smart, aggressive, resourceful companies distinguish themselves in sluggish industries. They can run mediocre competitors out of business or buy them out. In trendy industries (computers, the Internet, biotechnology), everybody's smart, aggressive, and resourceful, so those qualities can threaten an investment. When your favorite company makes an ingenious product, there's always a rival working overtime to make it better or sell it cheaper.

The way investors win in this inferior business is to buy the low-cost operators. That was the Buffett/Davis modus operandi all along. Both sought high-profit, well-managed insurers with minimal overhead, like **GEICO** and **AIG**. Inspired leadership was paramount. "You can get a lot of surprises in insurance," Buffett wrote. "[This business] tends to magnify, to an unusual degree, human managerial talent— or the lack of it. . . ."

Early on, Davis had identified the most critical factor: the proliferation of assets inside insurance company portfolios. The industry's bottom line was disappointing, but income from bonds, stocks, and mortgages increased from $330 million in 1951 to $38.8 billion in 1999. This remarkable increase made insurance investing worthwhile.

CHAPTER 8

CHRIS AND ANDREW BECOME IMMERSED IN THE BUSINESS

BORN IN THE 1960s, SHELBY'S THREE CHILDREN— Andrew, Chris, and Victoria ("Tory")—were introduced to stocks about the time the market began its tentative recovery from the 1973 to 1974 debacle. Between their father and grandfather, the young trio got a double dose of stock talk.

Andrew's enthusiasm was apparent in elementary school. When his teacher asked the class to write a report about the Pilgrims, he wrote about Memorex instead. The teacher told Shelby she'd never received an analyst's report from a fourth grader. Meanwhile, at Shelby's urging, the children opened savings accounts at the local bank in Tuxedo. Each deposited $25, one of their Christmas presents, in the Empire Savings Bank. This was their first lesson in the magic of compounding. Six years later—this was a period of high interest rates—they were astounded to discover their $25 had more than doubled.

Andrew doesn't remember being taught the Rule of 72, but he devised his own simplified version: "Going from $1 to $2 to $4 is okay, but going from $4 to $8 to $16 is terrific. Wait long enough, and the next double starts to make you wealthy."

By age 8, Andrew had learned that a savings deposit was a poor substitute for owning shares. Shelby encouraged the children to compound with their odd-job proceeds. To teach them the power of leverage, he matched their investment dollar for dollar.

After Andrew bought $800 worth of United Jersey Bank, Shelby set up a phone chat between the grade-school shareholder and the bank's investor relations officer. Andrew posed the questions and wrote down the answers. He wasn't sure what the answers meant, but the stock did well. He sold it at $12 and watched it rise to over $30—an early lesson in the annoyance of selling too soon. Still, he was impressed with his profit.

At age 10, Chris was already hip to the *great manager* theory of investing. He took a stake in an insurer, Associated Madison, after he found out Gerry Tsai was running that company. From hearing Shelby talk about the ex-go-go fund jockey, Chris figured Tsai was a high-powered celebrity. After he bought shares, Chris met a kid from Madison, Wisconsin, at a summer camp. "Does that Madison have anything to do with Associated Madison?" he asked the kid.

Both Chris and Andrew lost track of their early investments and don't recall what happened to their childhood assets. Chris figures the money is still out there, compounding in some forgotten brokerage account. In any event, they never complained about not touching their profit. They'd learned from Shelby and from their grandfather that spending, especially idle spending, was a regrettable habit.

Though his family lived comfortably, Andrew got the sense there was no cash around the house. He grew up hearing and hating the Davis frugality mantra, "Use it up, wear it out, make do or do without." The bus was his main form of transportation. He rarely saw the inside of a cab.

Shelby and Wendy divorced in 1975. Shelby took up with Gale Lansing, a portfolio assistant in his office. A tall, slim, no-nonsense type with a subtle sense of humor, Gale came from modest circumstances in a small town in upstate New York. On her first visit to Northeast Harbor, Gale was subjected to the Davis mountaineering test. Shelby took her up the Precipice, a 1,000-foot cliff studded with handholds and ladders. Gale was as cheery at the top as she'd been at the bottom.

Shelby and Gale had three children together, bringing Shelby's total to six. (The younger trio hadn't reached adulthood as of this writing, so I omitted them from this narrative.)

Without Wendy's Martha Stewartship, Shelby let the Tuxedo property fall into disrepair. He scrapped the formal garden—gardeners were too expensive. He heated with wood stoves to save energy, and he stopped heating unoccupied rooms. The money he saved on heating bills, he invested in his mutual fund. When he traveled in the summertime, he rented the house for extra income.

As a father, Shelby was a slightly mellower version of Davis—a stern and occasionally fun-loving taskmaster, generally absorbed in his work.

Shelby's overriding concern was that his children not be "spoiled." Whether they spent the night in a shack or a mansion, they were taught to appreciate the experience. They never dug a swimming pool, but they raked a lot of leaves and shoveled a lot of snow. One summer, they cleared enough milkweed from around the Tuxedo house to fill a grain silo. Being spoiled was closely related to spending, and "spender" continued to be the worst put-down in the family lexicon.

Shelby had grown up on big-band jazz and the stock market; his children grew up on rock and roll and the stock market. When they reached junior high, Shelby paid them $100 a pop to analyze companies. "The most important thing I taught them about the investment business," Shelby recalls, "is how I loved being in it, even in the lean years of the 1970s. I was convinced picking stocks was something any kid could do, and I tried to make it fun and keep it simple. The math part—accounting and spreadsheets—I figured they could learn later. I got them involved in the detective work, sniffing out clues about a company's prospects. Sometimes, I took them along on company visits, just like my father had taken me."

On a typical Saturday morning in Tuxedo, Shelby could be found perched in a basement cubicle, reading the contents of his briefcase. Every Friday night, he and the children watched Lou Rukeyser's show, *Wall Street Week,* on the black-and-white TV that sat on a kitchen countertop. *Wall Street Week* was followed by *Washington Week,* a second obligatory event. "We never talked about baseball, hockey, or Hollywood," Andrew recalls. "Just stocks and politics." He remembers hiking down a steep trail with Shelby in Acadia National Park in Maine, discussing earnings versus cash flow. "Although you might want to talk about other things with Dad, this was it."

On the school front, grades weren't as important to Shelby as where the grades were headed. He tracked academic progress the way he tracked corporate profits: He looked for an up trend. A student who started the year with straight As and ended with straight As didn't impress him as much as one who started with Cs and moved up to As. Chris, Andrew, and Tory tried to give him an advancing trend line.

Though all three children were immersed in Wall Street (they got an extra dose from their stepfather, who worked at a Manhattan brokerage house), they were sick of the subject by the end of high school. Tory, studied literature at Harvard, then medicine at Stanford. Andrew enrolled at Colby College in Maine, intending to major in psychology. The *Wall Street Journal* began to appear in his mailbox, but he hadn't ordered the paper, and assumed all students received a free subscription. In fact, Shelby had sent it incognito.

The steady supply of *Journals* helped rekindle Andrew's interest in the money game. He was always a hard worker. He split his summers between camps and jobs, including a two-month job at a small investment house, arranged by his stepfather. After his first year at Colby, he changed his major to economics and business. Andrew never considered applying for work with Shelby or with Davis. The family, he'd been told many times, was not an automatic employer, even as a last resort. Andrew followed in his footsteps and repeated Shelby's pattern. Shelby was hired out of college by The Bank of New York; Andrew was hired by Shawmut Bank in Boston. Shelby had apprenticed as an analyst in aluminum, rubber, steel, and other basic industries; Andrew apprenticed with PaineWebber's "commissioner" of steel.

In 1986, Andrew left Boston and Shawmut for New York and PaineWebber. He soon became the in-house expert in bond/stock hybrids known as "convertible securities"—or, in Wall Street parlance, "converts." A convert pays interest like a bond but offers its owner the possibility of capital gain if the company's common stock advances. A high-quality convert can capture 75 to 80 percent of the upside in a stock, while the bond feature limits its downside. Andrew created a 10-point rating system to aid comparison shopping in the group.

During a seven-year hitch at PaineWebber, Andrew moved quickly through the ranks to vice president. He became a star performer at the "shout downs"—daily briefings with 14,000 PaineWebber brokers listening to market advisories via a worldwide phone hookup.

Chris came to Wall Street by a more circuitous route. His grandfather was the primary inspiration. At age 15, he signed on as the Davis summer cook at the Maine house. The next summer, when he turned 16 and got his driver's license, Chris became the family chauffeur and drove the patriarch back and forth to the Bar Harbor airport.

During the school year, he worked weekends in Davis's office at 70 Pine Street, stuffing envelopes, typing the insurance letter, and sending messages on the Telex system that Davis never learned to operate. Grandson and grandfather developed a warm and easy give-and-take. They took walks together. They discussed politics, Wall Street, and why a frankfurter was an unnecessary extravagance.

"One day, we were passing by the vacant lot next to the office," says Chris. Later, J.P. Morgan built its new world headquarters on that lot, but at the time, it was a popular location for pushcart food vendors. "I asked my grandfather for a dollar to buy a hot dog. He said, 'Do you realize if you invest that dollar wisely it will double every five years? By the time you reach my age, in 50 years, your dollar will be worth $1,024. Are you so hungry you need to eat a $1,000 hot dog?' I guessed not. In one swoop, he taught me three lessons: the value of a dollar, the value of compound interest, and the importance of always carrying my own money."

Around this time, Chris defected to the communists. He wore a Lenin pin, touted Karl Marx, and quoted Chairman Mao instead of Warren Buffett.

A picture of Ché Guevara hung on Chris's bedroom wall—the political antidote to photos of Hoover, Dewey, Nixon, Ford, Kissinger, Reagan, Bush, and other GOP notables hanging on his grandfather's office wall, alongside numerous commendations and proclamations in parchment.

Chris loved animals. On summer vacations from high school, he worked at the Bronx Zoo, pro bono. He cleaned cages at the Humane Society clinic. Being an animal lover, he thought he'd make a good veterinarian. He attended prevet classes at Cornell University and planned to enroll as a full-time student, but a campus adviser suggested he take a year off and try something different. The University of St. Andrews in Scotland was recruiting Americans. Chris applied and was accepted. He'd planned to stay one year and ended up staying four. "Scotland," he said, "was love at first sight."

In Scotland, he discovered another type of love when he and a girlfriend lived together in a cottage on a sheep farm near the university. He managed to subsist on $8 a week: $4 for groceries, $4 for the occasional beer. He graduated with a master's degree in philosophy and theology, and found himself attracted to the priesthood.

After graduation, Chris worked as a pastoral assistant at the American Cathedral in Paris. A family friend from a church in Tuxedo Park, Father Leo (the very Reverend James Leo or Dean James Leo), was in charge of the cathedral. Chris slept on the floor of one of the cathedral's lofts. He leaned over the edge to answer the telephone, perched on a table a few feet below. Once he fell off, answering a call. No date could visit his "room" without walking past a huge crucifix.

Chris saw his grandfather when the latter came to Scotland to visit life insurance companies (the Scots' term is "life assurance"). The country was well supplied with flinty savers, dogged investors, and some of the earliest mutual funds on record. Various institutions, including the life assurers, had listened to Davis's advice and bought shares through his office.

That his grandson was pro-Mao, anti-Wall Street, and studying for the priesthood didn't ruffle Davis. He made jokes about it. "Philosophy and theology give you the perfect background for investing," he said. "To succeed at investing, you need a philosophy. Then you've got to pray like hell." On another occasion, Chris traveled to London to meet his grandfather for dinner. Davis was lodged in a reputable hotel; Chris stayed in a slummy flat where some of his radical friends had squatted. The dress code was a problem. Chris couldn't don his jacket and tie in front of his squat mates, and he couldn't enter the dining room at Davis's hotel in his radical rags. To avoid embarrassment in both places, he exited the slummy flat wearing the rags and hiding his capitalist uniform in a plastic trash bag. He planned to change outfits in the hotel's public bathroom, but a doorman refused to let him into the lobby. He sneaked around the building and came in through a side door.

Chris related the story during the meal. Davis was amused. He admired Chris's buddies for figuring out how to live rent-free in London. On the virtues of not spending money, the tycoon and the Marxist sympathizer could agree.

The pair hiked together in Switzerland, and Chris sat in on meetings between Davis and Swiss insurance executives. It was Davis and Shelby all over again, one generation removed.

Chris exited St. Andrews with a master's degree in theology, but Father Leo helped him realize he wasn't cut out for the priesthood. He'd already decided he wasn't cut out for veterinary work, so he moved back to the United States and took up residence in Boston. His mother's family was well-known in the city and his brother Andrew had apprenticed there.

Several rejections later, he applied for a job at Putnam, the Boston investment house, but couldn't land an interview. He schmoozed a secretary who told him if he showed up at 8:30 A.M., she'd arrange a chat with the boss, George Putnam. Chris got the chat, but not the job. He never mentioned he was Davis's grandson, even though he knew Davis and Putnam were old friends.

Shelby provided all three children a $500-a-month stipend, payable after they left college. This family "safety net" was enough to cover part of Chris's rent, but he couldn't live on $500 without employment. Hitting his grandfather for a loan was inconceivable—a man who refused to finance a $1 hot dog and lose $1,000 compounded over 50 years wasn't about to spring for a grocery allowance or a down payment on a car. Davis had always insisted: "You're getting nothing from me.

That way, you won't be robbed of the pleasure of earning it yourself."

Desperate for work by now, Chris scanned the classifieds in the *Boston Globe,* and found a training program at State Street Bank. Shelby advised that State Street's mutual fund business was exploding and the bank was in a hiring mode. Chris reminded himself that his father, his brother, and his stepfather all had trained at banks. Banking ran in the family.

After a few months of crunching the fund data, Chris was hired away by a small Wall Street boutique, owned and operated by Graham Tanaka. Before starting his own company, Tanaka had knocked around at J.P. Morgan and at Fiduciary Trust, where he'd worked with Shelby. Tanaka sought young talent; Shelby encouraged his son to apply. Chris got the job and moved to New York. By day, he worked for Tanaka as an analyst; by night, he took classes at the College of Insurance near the World Trade Center. One evening, when he was studying in the college library, he looked up from whatever he was reading and saw his grandfather's face on the wall. He quizzed the librarian and learned he was sitting in the Shelby Cullom Davis library. Davis had endowed it.

As Tanaka's insurance specialist, Chris attended meetings, visited companies, interviewed CEOs, and separated the doers from the bluffers. In late 1990, he ran into his father and his grandfather at a breakfast sponsored by the global insurer, Chubb. This was a momentous reunion: Three generations of Davises were attending the same meeting to get the latest details on the same company. None had a clue the others would be there.

During a coffee break in the hallway, Davis made his grandson an offer Chris couldn't refuse: "Come work for me," he said, "and keep an eye on things." Chris left Tanaka and moved to Davis headquarters on Pine Street.

CHAPTER 9

THE FAMILY
JOINS FORCES

ITH DAVIS SLOWING DOWN AND SHELBY considering his own retirement, the next generation was preparing a friendly takeover. They'd proven themselves at other firms (Andrew at PaineWebber; Chris at Tanaka), and now they were moving into the family financial fold.

Chris had quit Tanaka to work full time in his grandfather's office. (Their desks were just a few feet apart.) He noticed an old seersucker jacket draped over the back of Davis's chair. The blue stripes had faded; the white stripes had yellowed. Since Davis wore a newer jacket to work and never took it off, Chris wondered at the purpose of the sartorial relic. One day, he popped the question: "What's with that rag on the chair?"

"It's for the bank credit officers," Davis replied. "They come around to check on their margin loans. They arrive unannounced. If I'm not around to greet them, they'll suspect the boss is playing hooky and nobody's in charge. When they see the coat hanging on my chair, they think I just stepped out for coffee."

"How long has the coat been in that spot?"

"Twenty years."

When grandfather and grandson left the office for an analysts' meeting, Davis always jogged the distance, holding his suit jacket so it wouldn't flap in the breeze. An octogenarian jogger in a business suit was an entertaining sight. "If a customer sees me on the street, it's good for him to know I'm not lazying around," Davis explained.

Chris wrote a sample paragraph for Davis's weekly insurance bulletin. To his surprise, it appeared verbatim in the next edition. One paragraph became two, and soon Chris was writing the entire text. "I could tell my grandfather was relieved to be done with it," Chris said. Over a two-year period, he produced at least 50 letters. He changed the layout and omitted much of the industry data his grandfather had continued to print even after the latest numbers were accessible to any investor with a computer. He used the extra space to report on specific companies. The revamped format didn't generate reader response, any more than the old format had.

"Why do we bother with this?" he asked Davis, "when nobody reads it?"

"It's not for the readers," Davis said. "It's for us. We write it for ourselves. Putting ideas on paper forces you to think things through."

Chris learned, from his grandfather, not to take earnings at face value. Davis taught him how new life insurance sales built future prosperity while resulting in continuously reporting short-term losses, because commissions and marketing costs were deducted from earnings up front. An insurance policy that brought income to the company for the next 30 to 40 years went on the books as a debit.

Davis still commuted on the early train from Tarrytown, but he'd lost some pep. Little by little, the old man relinquished responsibility that Chris eagerly took on. After he got full control of the newsletter, Chris turned his attention to the few remaining "house accounts" that belonged to Davis's last remaining clients. He convinced his grandfather to charge a fee for managing these portfolios, as opposed to taking a commission on the rare occasion a stock was sold. Davis liked the idea and installed Chris as manager.

When his clients discovered that Davis had tapped his 25-year-old grandson (with no MBA) to handle their investments, they were politely unimpressed. "Why shouldn't they be wary?" Chris said. "I was untested, young, and related to the boss. But after a while, the results convinced them I wasn't just a nepotism hire. As for my lack of an MBA, neither my father nor my grandfather believed that degree was necessary, or even useful, in the investment business.

"The more responsibility my grandfather handed down, the more relaxed he became. I could see it on his face. Burdens were lifted."

One day in 1992, Davis approached Chris's desk carrying a blue binder big enough to hold oversized maps. Inside was a thick computer printout. Chris thumbed through the top pages and realized he was staring at his grandfather's career. Here were the gains and losses from a half-century of investing, alphabetized by company and displayed on green-and-white-striped paper. Chris had never seen the printout; he knew Shelby hadn't either. He felt it was equivalent to being invited into the studio of an artistic recluse who'd never shown his work in public.

"Look this over and make some recommendations about what to sell and what to keep," Davis said, matter-of-factly. "I'll go through it," Chris promised. He was amazed that his grandfather would seek an outside opinion, flattered to be asked, and uneasy that Davis hadn't asked Shelby instead. He wondered whether Davis wanted him to show the portfolio to

Shelby. Perhaps this was his grandfather's backhanded attempt to seek his estranged son's advice, or admiration, using Chris as a conduit.

After hours, Chris biked to his apartment with the printout stashed in his daypack. He decided to share it with Shelby, no matter what his grandfather's intent. That evening, he took the train to Tuxedo Park, where he and Shelby sat at the dining room table reviewing Davis's holdings, page by page. Shelby noticed more than a dozen stocks he'd owned and recommended.

Fiduciary Trust was there—Davis had bought shares after Fiduciary acquired his son's firm—Davis, Palmer and Biggs. Fannie Mae was there—a stock Shelby had owned and recommended since the early 1980s. New York Venture was there, so Davis had bought Shelby's mutual fund without having mentioned it. Intel was there—as a rule, Shelby avoided tech stocks, but this one impressed him so much Shelby had made it a top ten holding in the New York Venture Fund. He'd once touted Intel to his father and was rebuffed. "I don't trust technology," Davis had said.

Shelby didn't say so, but Chris could see he was touched by the evidence that Davis had secretly been taking Shelby's advice and investing in Shelby's favorite stocks—and in Shelby's fund. "Intel, Fannie Mae, and New York Venture."

Shelby and Chris spent the rest of the evening sifting through the pluses and minuses in this stockpicker's grab bag. Three-quarters of Davis's assets were riding on 100 insurers worldwide; the rest were scattered among 1,500 companies of all stripes and sizes. Most were highly ranked by Value Line. Why had he acquired so many names? Shelby explained that his father had never kicked the habit of buying in 1,000-share lots. "Charlie, get me 1,000," he'd say to his trader, even after his portfolio had grown beyond $100 million. With that much money involved, and to stay fully invested, he ended up own-ing 1,000 shares in enough companies to fill a small-town phone book.

The printout left no doubt what had put Davis on the *Forbes* list. It wasn't his phone book of stocks; it was a few names in the phone book. These were oldies from the 1960s that he had faithfully held—his financial Wyeths, Rauschen-bergs, Warhols. With the typical mutual fund turning over 100 percent of its inventory every year, and the public trading in and out of stocks and funds just as readily, Davis remained loyal. Names he owned in 1950 still occupied his portfolio in 1990.

His million shares of Hank Greenberg's American Interna-tional Group (AIG) were worth $72 million. Tokio Marine & Fire, the Japanese masterpiece that cost him $641,000 in 1962, was worth $33 million. Three other Japanese insurance hold-ings—Mitsui, Sumitomo Marine & Fire, and Yasuda Fire and Marine—were worth a combined $42 million.

Domestically, his second best investment, after Green-berg, was with Buffett. A 3,000-share purchase of Buffett's flagship company, Berkshire Hathaway, had grown into $27 million. He'd also parlayed five other U.S.-based insurers (Torchmark, AON, Chubb, Capital Holdings, and Progres-sive) into another $76 million. An additional $11 million had come his way (thanks to Shelby) via the mortgage packager, Fannie Mae.

This was the Davis Dozen—12 stocks worth $261 million, or, by today's accounting, at least two, and possibly three PowerBall jackpots. He won this prize on the original cash outlay of $150,000. The prize required a 50-year waiting pe-riod to accumulate, but Davis lived comfortably on small, an-ticipatory withdrawals along the way. Once he'd bought winning companies, his best decisions were never to sell. He sat on his insurance stocks through daily, weekly, monthly gyrations. He sat through mild bear markets and severe bear markets, crashes, and corrections. He sat through scores of analysts' upgrades and downgrades, technical sell signals, and fundamental blips. As long as he believed in the strength of the leadership and the company's continual ability to compound, he held.

Counting Buffett's company as an insurance play (Berkshire Hathaway was heavily invested in the sector), 11 of Davis's biggest winners were insurers. The lone outsider, Fannie Mae, resembled an insurer in that it was both a borrower and a lender, and it trafficked in mortgages and bonds.

Davis's intermediate winners (stocks that made him $4 to $9 million) were insurers as well. This list included St. Paul, CNA Financial, Hanover, Hartford Steam Boiler (which sold insurance policies for industrial furnaces); Kemper, Primerica, Safeco, 20th Century, U.S. Life, Conseco, and other names. The bottom line on this portfolio is: A few big winners are what count in a lifetime of investing, and these winners need many years to appreciate. All of the Davis Dozen had been parked in his portfolio since the mid-1970s. Any young, inexperienced investor has a built-in advantage over a mature, sophisticated investor: Time.

On the minus side of the ledger, Shelby and Chris found an ample assortment of flops, bombs, and wealth busters—or whatever other name fits stocks investors wish they'd never met. Among hundreds of losers, Davis's most expensive flop was First Executive, a persistent reverse compounder that turned his $2.5 million outlay into goose eggs. Not only had he refused to part with First Executive during its death spiral, he'd kept the corpse on the books.

In the final analysis, Davis's mistakes hindered his prosperity the way a gnat flusters a buffalo. His portfolio proved once again that, over a lifetime of investing, a handful of high achievers' ideas can support a multitude of ne'er-do-wells.

After they'd finished admiring the printout, Shelby and Chris discussed how they might prepare for the time when Davis was no longer capable of handling his affairs. There was no definite plan, but the general idea was to funnel Davis's assets into Shelby's New York Venture Fund, along with an array of new funds he soon would launch or acquire. Chris and Andrew, meanwhile, would be tapped to manage some of these newer portfolios, and if they performed well, they'd be qualified to run the expanded Davis operation. The accumulated wealth of two generations would now be left in the hands of the next, along with considerable assets from public shareholders.

In 1990, Saddam Hussein and his Keystone Kops army sacked Kuwait. The invasion that led to the Gulf War was bullish for oil prices but bearish for stocks. After breaking 3,000 for the first time, the Dow dropped 20 percent. The Tokyo market collapsed. Japan's Dow (the Nikkei) fell 48 percent. The Gulf war turned to rout, the U.S. economy went into short recession; the Fed cut rates, and stocks resumed their climb on a surge in corporate profits. Russia staged its second revolution of the century. Communism and Mikhail Gorbachev were ousted in 70 hours.

Hoping their portfolios would bring them a carefree retirement, U.S. baby boomers tossed billions into mutual funds. Their vigorous buying helped make the 1990s the best decade for stocks since the 1950s.

The 1991 recession was brief and relatively mild, but it strained the banking system. Banks were still enfeebled by the permissive lending of the late 1980s, when they'd financed too many malls, high rises, and fanciful corporate takeovers. Among the brand-name banks in distress, Citicorp was technically bankrupt. At least 40 other U.S. banks were in or close to the same fix.

Citicorp had been a bank that couldn't say "no." It said "yes" to Canadian laughingstock Robert Campeau and financed Campeau's Mittyesque takeover of the largest department store chains in America. It said "yes" to real estate speculators in overbuilt markets, at a time when the bank hadn't fully recovered from its earlier yeses to corrupt and debt-ridden Latin American regimes.

Toward the end of the 1980s, a glut in commercial real estate pushed this once-proud multinational into technical bankrupcy as "nonperforming assets"—a bankers' euphemism for loans-we-wish-we-hadn't made—reached 6 percent of total assets. Citicorp's insufficient loss reserves didn't begin to cover its bad loans. The stock fell from above $35 to below $10.

At that point, the bank was operating on "trace amounts" of capital. Had regulators played by the book, Citicorp would have faced government seizure and possible liquidation. Luckily for shareholders, Citicorp was put in the "too big to fail category." Regulators allowed it to stay in business, with federal oversight. In a "memorandum of understanding," the bank promised to consult with the Federal Reserve and the Office of the Comptroller of the Currency on all consequential decisions.

Citicorp's pestiferous chairman, John Reed, didn't appreciate the unsolicited advice, but at least his bank was spared dismemberment. Soon, a Kuwaiti oil sheik came to the rescue with a huge bailout loan. The Gulf War, fought to protect Kuwaiti oilfields, also helped keep the biggest U.S. bank afloat.

Banking problems and Saddam's bear market gave Shelby his latest chance to prospect in familiar territory. Like everyone else who read the business section and watched financial TV, he'd heard influential alarmists predict the demise of Citibank and escalating real estate loan losses for Wells Fargo. The prices of both Citi's and Wells's stock reflected their predicaments. Refusing to take somebody else's word for it, and convinced that the Fed wouldn't allow a top-notch bank to fail (already, Fed chairman Alan Greenspan had cut short-term rates), Shelby quizzed the horses, as usual.

The answers reassured him. Insiders at Wells Fargo told Shelby their loan problems weren't as problematic as headlines suggested. The bank had moved into Southern California, hoping to benefit from that state's fast growth. It beat many competitors into supermarkets with ATM machines. In Wells Fargo's chairman, Carl Reichardt, he found the kind of no-nonsense leader that had inspired Davis to make his best investments. "Shelby, I've got $50 million of my own money in this institution," Reichardt told him. "I won't let you down." When Wells merged with Norwest, it inherited two more top managers, Dick Korvasovich and Les Biller.

With slight trepidation, Shelby loaded up on shares of Wells. So he wouldn't be caught off guard by unpleasant surprises, he kept close tabs on the latest developments. "At night, I'd wake up worrying about some detail, and the next day, I'd call to check. I talked to them at least twenty times in six months. Gradually, I was more convinced they had their problems under control."

Here's another tidbit from the Great Investors Think Alike department: Warren Buffett was also buying Wells. Just as Buffett and Davis had owned the same insurance companies, Buffett and Shelby favored the same bank.

That two great investors were bullish didn't faze the short-selling Feshbach brothers. Wall Street's most famous pessimists bet heavily against Wells. Miscalculations on the short side cost them their Lear jet and their billion dollars under management.

Citi was in worse shape than Wells, but Shelby was impressed with its global franchise. On a family trip to the Far East, when Shelby was a teenager, he'd met the head of Citi's Burmese branch. He likened the bank to an embassy, with operatives in every country. Now, 40 years later, he favored globetrotting companies, and Citi's crisis gave him a chance

116

to steal one. Though its foolish lending habit, especially in the Third World, had nearly cost Citi its corporate life (doing business abroad was no cinch), Shelby figured U.S. banking authorities wouldn't allow it to fail. In an effort to cut back on costly generosity, Citi's bosses had tightened the purse strings in the lending department. Also, they'd hired a "brand promoter" to help Citicorp—renamed Citigroup—capitalize on its fame.

By the end of the decade, Shelby's Citi investment had advanced twentyfold, and he'd acquired more shares after the merger with Travelers. (The New York Venture Fund already owned Travelers.) The new Citigroup entity was run by Sandy Weill, Travelers CEO and another Davis-style leader. Weill was one more example of how a great leader can take a company farther than any data cruncher could fathom. Like Greenberg at AIG, Weill's mission was to "acquire, grow, and cut costs." He accomplished all three and kept his promise of doubling Citigroup's earnings every five years.

Impressed with Chris's success with the house accounts, Shelby installed Chris as manager of the new Davis Financial Fund in 1991. With the banking crisis still in the news and the entire sector irresistibly cheap, Chris could apply his stock-picking skills to the sector. Financial services already had begun to benefit from baby boomers' squirreling for retirement, just as insurance companies benefited when the baby boomers' parents bought policies after World War II.

"A general fund couldn't have owned 90 percent financials," Chris said. "I wanted to be able to concentrate. If I made a good showing, it might put me in line to manage the New York Venture Fund after my father retired. The Davis board of directors handles such decisions, and I wanted to prove myself to the board."

Using the family's invest-in-great-leaders technique, Chris picked a winner in Eli Broad's insurance company, SunAmerica.

Thirty years earlier, Shelby's partner, Jeremy Biggs, had lent venture capital to Broad's home-building operation, Kaufman & Broad. Broad and his associates put 2,000 residential developments on the map, selling mostly to baby boomers. Broad was now selling financial products to the same people who had bought his houses. SunAmerica proceeded to capture $50 billion in retirement assets. Based on Chris's analysis, Shelby made SunAmerica one of New York Venture Fund's top picks, and the stock proceeded to rise twentyfold.

The life of a mutual fund isn't as dull as it might sound. A $1 billion fund with an average turnover (100 percent) buys and sells $1 billion worth of inventory each year. Managers with average longevity have owned enough companies to fill a small town's phone book. Some companies are acquired once and then dumped for good; others are owned, disowned, and acquired again. The managers regret having sold some companies, and they regret having bought others. Writers may balk at rereading their earliest work; actors may prefer not to watch their old movies; and fund managers may avoid contemplating their mistakes.

Chris's biggest rookie mistake was to urge his father to kick Fannie Mae out of the Fund. Shelby took his son's advice and Fannie Mae proceeded to mock the decision by quadrupling in price.

In their off hours, Shelby and Chris planned the gradual liquidation of Davis's holdings. Shelby wanted to sell some of the poor companies first, to create tax losses that would offset gains from the sale of winners. "Spring housecleaning," Shelby called it. Chris broached the subject with Davis. "I mentioned housecleaning one day," Chris said, "emphasizing the part about the tax breaks to play on my grandfather's loathing of taxes. I didn't mention that my father thought some of these stock picks were misguided to begin with. To bring that up was like squirting charcoal starter on a grass fire.

"Screwing up my courage, I asked my grandfather point-blank how he wanted us to handle his portfolio when he died. His answer surprised me. 'I want my money invested in the Davis funds,' he announced. He'd already concluded that leaving his portfolio intact with Shelby in charge was a fool-hardy strategy because, in that case, poor performance might go unpunished. With the money in the funds, a board of directors would safeguard the assets. If Shelby failed to deliver, or his successors failed to deliver, the directors could find new managers."

Chris relayed this conversation to his father, and, soon after, the three generations openly conferred on the transfer of assets. Poor companies were unloaded immediately, and the bulk of the portfolio was slated for sale after Davis's death.

Meanwhile, the New York Venture Fund continued to out-perform its rivals and outdistance the market, and Shelby's roster of funds expanded. He took control of three funds purchased from a subsidiary of Lincoln National Life, and re-named them Davis Growth Opportunity, Davis High Income, and Davis Tax-Free Income. He hired a new manager for each. Later, two additional funds—Selected American and Se-lected Special Shares—fell into his lap. After an in-house squab-ble over fees and commissions, the powers-that-be at Selected sacked the former management group (Kemper) and switched to Shelby. Shelby wasted no time replacing unproductive con-sumer stocks with banks, insurance, and brokerage names.

Among powers-that-be, other founding partners had owned a 55 percent stake in the Fund's management company. Shelby offered to buy them out. With money he'd saved by living in a Greenwich Village walk-up, Chris invested in the buyout as well. Venture Advisers became Davis Selected Advisers, and the family was now in full control; Shelby operated from the World Trade Center, and Chris from his new location on Fifth Avenue. Following the migration of Morgan Stanley,

PaineWebber, and other financial gorillas, Chris closed his grandfather's Pine Street office and moved uptown. To keep the Davis tradition intact, Chris brought along his grandfather's furniture, VIP photographs, and citations, and installed them in the conference room at the modest new offices.

By 1993, Chris's brother Andrew had quit PaineWebber, frustrated that younger employees had trouble rising through the old-boy network. Impressed with Andrew's success in the convertible bond department at PaineWebber, Shelby decided to start a convertible fund to showcase Andrew's talent, just as he'd done with Chris and the financial fund. While he was at it, Shelby also put Andrew in charge of a new real estate fund, since a major slump in commercial property made real estate stocks attractive.

In their new managerial roles, Chris and Andrew were picking stocks in a market that wasn't the cheap, down trodden variety that Davis had encountered in 1947, nor the extravagant, hyperbolic variety that Shelby had encountered in 1969, though it was closer to the latter than to the former.

Soon, Andrew was absorbed in getting the scoop on scores of real estate companies, many of which had recently gone public. He moved his family to Santa Fe, where he tended both portfolios and also kept tabs on administrative matters. Andrew was two time zones away from Chris, who managed the more prestigious financial fund, worked more closely with his father, was chummier with his grandfather, and stood first in line to replace Shelby as manager of the New York Venture Fund. One weekend in 1993, he and Chris met at a Colorado ski resort to talk through this apparently unequal distribution of responsibility, notoriety, and clout. Andrew told Chris he wasn't bothered that Chris had landed the higher-profile assignment. The brothers promised each other they'd maintain an honest dialogue to ward off future misunderstandings.

On a ski trip to Switzerland in the spring of 1993, Davis refused to ski. There was a strange hitch in his walk. Alarmed at these developments (Davis never missed a chance to ski), Kathryn sent him to a doctor when they returned to the States.

Kathryn drove him straight to Columbia-Presbyterian Medical Center on Riverside Drive in Manhattan. An emergency room doctor said Davis had suffered a stroke and admitted him for observation. Kathryn booked a room in the luxury wing, which provided live chamber music and afternoon tea served in the garden. Davis was confined to a bed and a wheelchair. He must have felt very ill; he accepted the first-class accommodations. After two weeks of rehab, he limped out of the hospital against doctor's orders to attend a Value Line board meeting.

The family handled the stroke with its usual gritty aplomb. The Davis approach to injury, infirmity, or disability was "Don't give in to it." After Diana's husband, John Spencer, was stricken with multiple sclerosis, his in-laws continued to invite him on ski trips. Dad was always very empathetic to John about the plight of his M.S. He had a very caring side.

Davis took short walks but needed the wheelchair as a backup when he got tired. His doctors suggested more rehab, but Kathryn insisted on taking him and the wheelchair to Russia. The Davises had signed up for a boat trip up the Volga River on Boris Yeltsin's yacht, and, stroke or no stroke, Kathryn was sticking to the plan although she asked Chris to come along as well.

By summer's end, Davis wobbled more and remembered less. He was readmitted to Columbia-Presbyterian—weakened, disturbed, mentally confused, and angry at his condition and the fuss it was causing. In the hallway outside his grandfather's room, Chris watched his grandmother cry. It was the first time he'd ever seen her break down. "I'm afraid," she said, "our best days are behind us." Chris took it as a positive she'd come to this conclusion at age 84. "If that's the first time you've noticed your best days are behind you," he said, "then you've had a wonderful life."

With Davis incapacitated, Kathryn took over the Davis seat on the New York Stock Exchange. She was (and, as of this writing, still is) the oldest woman member of the exchange. When he bought the seat in 1940, Davis needed a partner for legal reasons. He tapped his wife. Kathryn didn't mind being listed as Davis's spousal stamp and serving in name only. She had no more interest in the NYSE than she had in the NFL. She hadn't visited the exchange in 40 years.

In early 1994, a family doctor advised Kathryn to transfer her husband to a warm climate. Shelby had bought a vacation home on Florida's Hobe Sound, a low-key millionaires' rookery north of Palm Beach, and he urged his mother to rent a place near his. Davis had always disliked the flat topography of Florida, but Kathryn agreed that the sunshine might be beneficial, so she followed Shelby's suggestion.

Davis suffered more strokes. His spirits got a lift when Shelby showed him the latest investment results. It had taken Davis 42 years to make the first $400 million. Shelby's mutual funds helped him make the next $500 million in four years. Had Davis switched his assets to the New York Venture Fund earlier, he'd have made a lot more.

The family lingered in Florida through the spring. Kathryn had flown to Massachusetts to attend a trustees' meeting at Wellesley College when she got word that Davis was close to death. She flew back with her daughter Diana to keep vigil at his bedside; other family members drifted in and out. When Chris arrived, he walked through the door and saw Shelby sitting on the bed, patting Davis's hand in reassurance, telling him everything would be okay. "I was touched by this scene," Chris said. "It was the most tender physical contact I'd ever witnessed between my father and grandfather." Davis died on May 24, 1994, at age 85.

The family struggled with funeral plans, given Davis's oft-stated opinion that funerals were a waste of time. When asked what sort of send-off he'd want, Davis always said: "None. My friends are much too busy for such nonsense." Kathryn and Shelby figured a way to finesse his objection (not that Davis was in any condition to object) by staging the ceremony in downtown New York at lunch time, so the mourners could pay their respects without taking time off from work.

St. Paul's Chapel, close to Wall Street, was the obvious choice.

The patriotic societies he loved and supported paid tribute by sending 75 flag bearers into the chapel. Sad strains from a lone bagpiper could be heard all the way down Wall Street. Chris gave a moving speech, quoting from his grandfather. Kathryn had written an eight-word eulogy: "He was my closest friend for 65 years." Diana spoke of her father citing examples of how he instilled her with a work ethic. A reception was held at the Downtown Association, Davis's favorite club.

Davis left a widow, two children, eight grandchildren, and $900 million, later to become more than $2 billion. He was cremated in Florida and his ashes were shipped to Maine. The family buried the urn in a glade at the edge of the property and installed a memorial bench.

Since the Davis estate was earmarked for charity, the remains of the portfolio could be liquidated free of capital gains taxes. The assets now belonged to the Davis charitable trust, controlled by a family board.

Davis left nothing to Shelby. Diana did receive $5 million—in today's dollars. Shelby's firm got more assets to manage in their mutual funds, but he got nothing directly. Following his father's lead, Shelby warned his six children not to expect any windfall from him. Entering his "return" phase, Shelby made a

$45 million donation to the United World College scholarship program and set up a $150 million foundation. He supported the programs on their own merits, but these endeavors were also a "message to my offspring. Don't plan to coast through life on the family fortune."

With no tax bill to worry about, Shelby accelerated the selling from his father's portfolio. He diverted the cash into the various Davis funds. Shelby, who'd worked hard to make money for thousands of small investors, was now making it for his father's favorite causes.

"Having so much Davis money in the funds helped us keep priorities straight," Chris said. "We cared less about bringing in more investors and more about doing well for existing investors. It's because we were the biggest existing investors, by far. If stocks in the fund rose 1 percent, the Davis family and our related charities benefited far more than we'd benefit by attracting another $10 million in clients' money."

In a bold and unsentimental maneuver, Shelby unloaded his father's beloved Japanese insurers. What went around came around: Shelby saw a striking resemblance between Japan in the 1990s and the United States in the 1930s. Both economies had stalled, and consumers were short on funds and afraid to spend money. Interest rates dropped to record lows—in Japan's case, below 2 percent. Low rates bedeviled insurers. Their bond portfolios didn't throw off enough cash to pay claims and/or benefits to policyholders.

The 1930s—and, to a slightly lesser extent, the 1970s—had shown that it often takes years, perhaps decades, for a market to recover from a devastating loss. So far, there was no hint of Japan's economic recovery, and waiting for a comeback, Shelby concluded, was a futile exercise. Seeing better opportunities at home in 1994 (just as his father had seen better opportunities abroad in 1963), Shelby said *sayonara* to Japan and sank the proceeds into U.S. stocks, just in time to catch Wall Street's latest 300 percent rise.

After guiding Davis Financial through four years of above-average returns, Chris was elevated, in 1995, to comanager of the New York Venture Fund. He put in long days doing research. A reporter described him as "having the glassy eyes of the sleep-deprived."

Andrew's real estate fund had distinguished itself from 1994 to 1997. Then an apparent glut in office space and shopping malls caused investors to retreat from the sector, in anticipation of a bust. Much of the retreating cash was deployed in a hotter sector: technology. Demoralized and doubting his commitment, Andrew sought his father's counsel, expecting Shelby to pass along some profound advice about coping with bear markets, such as the one Shelby had survived in 1973 to 1974. He got three words: "Hang in there." It wasn't the message Andrew had expected, but later he realized it was the only sensible response a veteran could give. In the first year of the twenty-first century, real estate rebounded with double-digit gains, providing a rewarding alternative to double-digit losses in tech stocks.

CHAPTER 10

CHRIS AND
NEW YORK
VENTURE FUND

CHRIS DAVIS TOOK OVER AS PORTFOLIO MANAGER of the New York Venture Fund in 1997, after having performed research closely alongside Shelby since 1990, the sixteenth year of the latest bull market. Over this remarkable stretch, Mr. Market's earnings—the E in the P/E calculation—were up fourfold. The price (P) had done even better, up more than eightfold. Investors in the Dow who paid a 7 multiple at the dawn of the advance—reluctantly, in many cases—now eagerly paid a 20 multiple in the twilight.

Shelby exited on a remarkable winning streak. Not only had his fund beaten the S&P 500 in 16 out of 20 years, he'd beaten the index by an annual 4.7 percent throughout this period. An original $10,000 investment had become $379,000.

Shelby gave himself a new title: Senior Research Advisor. "Chris is the quarterback," he said. "I'm the coach." To underscore this change of roles, Chris gave him a jacket that read "Coach." Chris was the same age as Shelby was when the New

York Venture Fund was launched. He had proven himself and had earned his place at the helm. Father and son met every week or so, and they talked constantly on the phone.

The backdrop for Chris's soloing with the New York Venture Fund bore an unsettling resemblance to the backdrop in 1969, when Shelby took charge. Then, fewer than 400 stock funds were operating in the United States. Now, with no birth control practiced in mutual funds, Wall Street's incubators had created 5,000 alternatives on the equity side alone. A record 45 percent of U.S. households had cash riding on this bull into the thin air of valuation. Stock ownership had never been higher, and Americans' personal savings had never been lower.

The hoopla in 1969 was directed toward computer peripherals, mainframes, or companies with names ending in "-ionics." Now, it was directed at dot-coms, B to B, C to C, chip makers, networking, and connectivity. Yesterday's go-go operatives (Gerry Tsai, Fred Mates, and similar headliners) were now replaced by "momentum" managers and thirty something Internet wonders like Ryan Jacobs. As described in the *New York Observer,* Jacobs was catapulted into the driver's seat of the nation's first mutual fund for Internet stocks. Prior to this unexpected job offer, Jacobs had worked as a reporter for a relatively obscure newsletter: *IPO Value Monitor.* In a hot market, people, as well as stocks, can be elevated to improbable heights.

This opportunistic fund, a home-grown concoction with 20 shareholders and $200,000 in assets, was launched by a brother of one of Jacobs' friends. Jacobs' hand was on the *Buy* button just in time to satisfy the Internet mania, and, in 1998, he wowed the Street with a 196 percent return. This result caused a buying scramble and a torrent of paperwork as new money poured into the fund's headquarters—a house in Babylon, Long Island. Jacobs made the cover of *Kiplinger's* magazine and was the subject of numerous adulatory articles.

By 1999, the Internet fund had swelled to $500 million. Like Gerry Tsai during an earlier era, Jacobs decided he'd attracted enough of a following to bolt the parent company. He quit his friend's brother's shop and set up his own: the Jacobs Fund. Investors laid a quick $150 million on the tyro, and higher stock prices and more investors quickly doubled those assets. Then, in the Internet crash of Y2K—seers had predicted that computers would break down, but computer stocks broke down instead—the Jacobs Fund lost a third of its former self, and the earlier client rush to join became a rush to resign.

The *Observer* reported late in 2000, that Jacobs believed his Internet picks would rally. What he couldn't quite believe was how, with no prior experience, he got his own mutual fund at age 30.

The same unconditional love that was delivered to "data" and "-ionic" stocks in the late 1960s was applied to dot-coms and Silicon Valley start-ups in the late 1990s. In the late 1960s, value guru Ben Graham issued warnings about market excess and was dismissed as a hoary crank; in the late 1990s, Graham's student, Warren Buffett, issued similar warnings and got the same brush-off. In 1965, Fed chairman William McChesney Martin chided the zealots for proclaiming the "new era" when recessions were passe and stock market fundamentals no longer applied. The last new era, Martin reminded, was the 1920s.

A quarter century later, Martin's cryptic, rumple-suited successor, Alan Greenspan, cried "Irrational exuberance," as did Warren Buffett at the Berkshire Hathaway annual meeting that year. After a reflex lapse, the Dow proceeded to add 2,000-plus points to its already bloated self. In sum, the late 1960s and the late 1990s were the best of times for cockeyed optimists and the worst of times for wary shoppers. Value-oriented funds (the New York Venture Fund among them) fell behind as hell-bent growth funds raced ahead. Several notable old-school managers, including Bob Sanborn at Oakmark and Julian Robertson at Tiger Management, quit the business outright. In 1999, Buffett's company had its worst year on record. The fogy himself, celebrated as money's Merlin as recently as 1995, was sent to the metaphoric nursing home by journalist Michael Lewis, author of the *New New Thing,* a book about a Silicon Valley instant billionaire. Lewis penned a *New York Times* column that chided some Old, Old Things, namely financial has-beens such as Buffett, Robertson, and George Soros.

In these Soaring 1990s, a standard household routine was to pay bills with debt (maxing out on credit cards and home equity loans), then funnel extra cash into the can't-lose tech sector. This was an anti-Davis maneuver—instead of saving to invest more, people invested to save less. Wishful thinking convinced them that their borrow-and-plunge strategy would finance a comfortable retirement *and* give them instant gratification along the way. In 2000, Mr. Market destroyed this illusion. Stocks had gotten far ahead of their 10 to 11 percent average annual reward, and the tech sector underwent a quick and violent regression to the mean. Belatedly, losers realized that the best investment they could have made was paying off their unpaid credit card balances.

Chris was six years older and considerably more experienced than Jacobs. The New York Venture Fund held its own and then some against its value-oriented peers in 1997 to 1999, but Mr. Market outran the value crowd, and tech was the booster.

"We're running a marathon, not a sprint," Chris said. "So it was a bit unnerving to be second-guessed on short-term performance. The whole money management business was fixated on the short-term. Consultants, magazines, rating systems were geared to what you did this week, this month, this quarter. If you underperformed for six months—or, God forbid—two years, you were in trouble."

"Following in the family tradition," says Chris, "I'm in business to defeat the S&P 500 index over time." So was every other fund manager on the planet, although for two decades this goal had eluded 75 percent of the managerial population. The question became: Why did millions of investors continue to pay proven losers to deploy their capital with below-average results? Under Shelby, the New York Venture Fund consistently beat the average, but in 1998 and 1999, Chris and the value crowd had no chance against reckless euphoria.

Chris promoted in-house analyst Ken Feinberg to share responsibility as the Fund's co-manager. Ken was the detail man, the micro to Chris's macro. "I never cared about building my own empire," Chris says. "I'd always admired Ken's work. I liked having somebody to bounce ideas off of, somebody who could share the research. Ken and I agreed we'd never buy anything without talking to him. My father's a tremendous filter. He's known many of these companies for decades."

Before Chris began managing the Fund, he had noticed that popular performance ratings didn't necessarily tell a useful story. "Everybody in the business is accustomed to keeping score with one-, three-, and five-year results," he said, "but the scoring system implies a consistency that isn't really there. For instance, let's say I lagged the market four years in a row, and then, in the fifth year, I was up 200 percent. I'd get a great five-year score, even though the fund had only one great stretch.

"Fund rankings can also mislead. Let's say a fund's return puts it in the top 10 percent for ten years, top 25 percent for five years, and top 50 percent for one year. This progression makes it look like the manager lost his touch. While his portfolio may be out of favor temporarily, the strategy that put him in the top ten for ten years is still intact. But the data don't show that.

"In the same vein, a fund could rank thirtieth out of 100 similar competing funds every year for three decades, and still end up number one for the entire period. As other short-term wonders move down in the rankings, a consistent performer moves up."

To Chris, the truest test of stockpicking talent is the "rolling return," which tracks a fund over a succession of five- or ten-year periods. Someone following New York Venture Fund's rolling return, for instance, would look at results from 1969 to 1979, then 1970 to 1980, then 1971 to 1981, and so on.

At the start of the long bull market, investors could buy Mr. Market for 10 to 15 times earnings, so thousands of stocks were in the Davis ballpark. When Chris got involved, Mr. Market was selling for 25 to 30 times earnings, and the Davis ballpark was far less crowded. It was harder to find a proven high achiever with a promising future and a value price, unless some bad press or a disappointing quarterly result caused the Street to ditch the stock. Chris and Ken took advantage of the fact that, late in this bull phase, Mr. Market had gotten the shakes, or in brokers' lingo, "increased volatility."

"In a recent stretch," Chris recalled, "the stock prices of 32 of our top 40 holdings moved up and down more than 50 percent between their lowest low and their highest high. And 15 of these stocks vacillated 100 percent." The shakes were disconcerting to an owner, but inviting to a potential buyer. Companies that Chris and Ken liked, except for their prices, suddenly became buys. An analyst at Morningstar, a mutual fund research service, called the New York Venture Fund "a rehab center for fallen growth stocks."

During the Fen-Phen crisis, drug maker American Home Products faced a multibillion-dollar liability over allegedly fatal side effects from the diet pill. Believing that "the stock price more than discounted the likely outcome" of the lawsuits, the duo bought American Home at a relatively safe and sane price. They also bought a high-flying conglomerate, Tyco, after SEC sleuths launched an investigation of accounting "irregularities." Along with associate Adam Seessel, Ken did a thorough number crunch and convinced himself (and Chris) that the SEC was on a snipe hunt.

In the Fund's semiannual report, Chris and Ken told their shareholders that American Home and Tyco were "illustrative of our willingness to purchase companies opportunistically while others are anxiously selling." They picked up Costco and Tellabs during similar sell-offs.

Their crisis surfing didn't always gratify. Chris and Ken resisted buying $80 Lucent until Mr. Market gave them the chance to own it at $60. The new owners watched Lucent drop into the $20s. "We thought we paid a reasonable amount, but the company used some creative accounting to fluff up the earnings." Still, Chris and Ken saw less risk in buying disparaged and fundamentally attractive companies after a markdown than in overpaying for celebrated and fundamentally attractive companies.

Creative accounting wasn't limited to Lucent. Chris discovered that many companies were fluffing their books to meet Street expectations and create an illusion of predictable success. Earnings were less and less what they appeared to be, so the most important measure of corporate merit was no longer reliable. The same fluffery had occurred near the top of the rise in Bull II, when Shelby was making his managerial debut. Shareholders didn't complain and regulators didn't investigate until after the market imploded. "I expect the same will happen after the next bear market," said Chris, "when the accountants' bag of tricks will be exposed."

A typical fund manager moved in and out of stocks at a frenzied pace—trading away every year, the portfolio's entire value and then some. The Davises remained boringly steadfast. Still the biggest clients of their own products, they minimized taxes by keeping a lid on the selling. Then, in 2000, the market momentum caused Chris and Ken to do a lot of uncharacteristic selling. Instead of waiting for companies to earn their way into higher valuations, investors bid them up in advance. Many stocks left the range of fair value and reached target prices the comanagers hadn't expected to see until 2005. Why wait for a prosperous hereafter if the hereafter has prematurely arrived? With that question in mind, they reduced their holdings in Texas Instruments and Applied Materials.

They also cut back on the banking sector, keeping their favorites (Wells Fargo, Fifth Third), but scuttling the Bank of America. Across the industry, profits were squeezed by higher interest rates. Delinquent loans were up; revenues were flat. In the insurance sector, they sold Chubb and Allstate. In the brokerage sector, they kept DLJ and Morgan Stanley Dean Witter. They held onto Wells Fargo, Citicorp, J.P. Morgan, Morgan Stanley, and AIG.

To Chris's grandfather, a stock was forever. Davis sold a few companies along the way, but his biggest winners were eternal holds. Shelby held onto AIG through most of his career, but he owned relatively few forever stocks. Though only time will tell the outcome, Chris picked American Express, McDonald's, Wells Fargo, AIG, and Buffett's Berkshire Hathaway as possible forever candidates.

Chris sees promise in multinational companies that can allocate capital around the world, wherever the best return can be earned. In the German, Japanese, and other foreign markets, he sees opportunity as more businesses follow America's lead and streamline their operations. Though he avoids Internet investments per se, he looks for the beneficiaries of Internet shopping and banking. American Express and Citicorp are two obvious examples.

"There's no investor who argues what he's buying is overvalued," Chris told a reporter, wading into the endless growth–value debate. "That's what investing is—trying to realize value." The two sides differ. Value investors seek to buy earnings at a reasonable price (although "reasonable" is open to interpretation). Growth investors will pay an apparently exorbitant price for a future earnings bonanza. Embryonic growth companies with zero earnings are bid up in anticipation of spectacular results ahead. In every promising start-up, investors hope to find the next Microsoft, Wal-Mart, Cisco, or Home Depot.

Given the fortunes that fast-growing companies like Microsoft have made for their founders, you'd think the high-priced, fast-growth camp would have landed a few stock pickers on the *Forbes* 400 richest Americans list. Yet no billionaires or near-billionaires have materialized from that group. Davis and Buffett got to ten figures from the value camp. They bought growth at modest prices.

The Nifty Fifty is a case study in the perils of high-priced growth. After the bears mauled the tech sector in 1969 to 1970, investors fled to the presumed safety of America's most esteemed enterprises. From Coca-Cola to Pfizer, Merck to McDonald's, Disney to American Express, the fleeing horde paid top dollar for quality. Most Nifties are far bigger and more profitable today than they were in 1970, so as growth companies they succeeded. But as top-dollar investments, they didn't live up to the price tag.

Wharton Professor Jeremy Siegel put a positive spin on the Nifties in his book, *Stocks for the Long Run*. According to Siegel, if you bought all 50 at peak prices in 1970, ignored your huge paper losses, and stuck with the portfolio, your loyalty was rewarded by 30 years later. At that point, the patient Nifties investor had caught up to the S&P 500.

Siegel's argument cheered up the growth camp because it vindicated the pricetag-be-damned growth stock strategy. Then astute reporters at *Barron's* magazine poked two big holes in Siegel's contention:

1. What investor was stubborn enough to ignore the initial 70 to 80 percent decline in his or her holdings and carry the Nifties through seven Presidential administrations? Families could raise kids and see them graduate from college before the Nifties paid off.
2. To get Siegel's result, you had to "rebalance" the portfolio every year by subtracting money from the winners and adding it to the losers. If you held the shares you bought in the first place, the Nifties returned about 2 percent a year. A passbook savings account was more rewarding.

Thus, owning some of the finest companies in the world was a lousy deal if you overpaid and a worse deal if you bought the most expensive Nifties. Companies with lower P/E ratios, such as Gillette and Disney, did better than those with higher ratios, such as Polaroid and Xerox, which never reached their former lofty prices again.

"Owning slower growth (8 to 14 percent) can be tremendously profitable if you don't overpay for it," Chris said. "But the Street aims for faster growth. Piles of analysts' reports land on my desk, and no matter what company is being analyzed or what product it sells, the conclusion is almost always the same: The long-term growth rate will equal or exceed 15 percent. With that in mind, I give friends, analysts, and other fund managers the following quiz: How many of the great Nifty Fifty companies grew their earnings at 15 percent, or better, from then to now?

"Knowing the Nifty list included Coke, Merck, IBM, Disney, and other outstanding performers, most people answer: '20 or 30 companies.' Or, if they try to give a low-ball response, they say: '10 or 15.' The real answer is three: Philip Morris, McDonald's, and Merck. This trio is the exception that proves an important point. It's unrealistic to expect companies to grow at 15 percent for extended periods. Most great companies can't do it. People who pay high prices for stocks, based on high growth assumptions, are asking for trouble up the line."

That's why the Davises, Peter Lynch, and Warren Buffett generally have avoided tech stocks. They've all made jokes about being technophobic, and Lynch admitted he was all thumbs with anything more sophisticated than a push-button phone. But the real cause of their avoidance is: Tech businesses aren't predictable. "Who could tell," Shelby said, "which of the dot-com companies would thrive, or even survive, over time? In other industries that transformed the country, from autos to airplanes, most of the pioneering companies' industries are no longer in business today."

In 1999, Chris heard Warren Buffett tell an audience he expected stocks to return 6 percent a year for the next 17 years—less than half the payoff during the prior 17 years. Buffett based this sobering forecast on simple math: In 1999, the entire lineup of Fortune 500 companies was selling for $10 trillion, supported by $300 billion in annual earnings. When the annual fees shareholders paid to own those assets—roughly, 1 percent of $10 trillion, or $100 million—were subtracted the actual payoff from their investing was $200 million. Contemporary investors were buying Mr. Market for 50 times earnings. Because an entire economy can't justify a multiple, of 50, Buffett surmised, stock prices would have to give. They might give slowly or give quickly, or meander until the nation's earnings caught up to them, but they couldn't rise at their former pace without violating the laws of financial gravity. A $3 trillion price tag on a market with $200 billion earnings might be reasonable—but $10 trillion? No way.

High valuations in the turn-of-the-century market caused Shelby to turn cautious as well. In the summer of 1998, he worried about the Asian financial mess in general, and Japanese bank failures in particular. His sidekick, Jeremy Biggs, had sighted a huge flock of construction cranes in Shanghai on a trip to the Far East. "Cranes on the skyline are a sign of a market top," Shelby said. He worried that the Japanese public would lose its life savings because Japan lacks deposit insurance. He fretted over unsold merchandise piling up in Chinese warehouses. "You sort of wonder if China will be forced to devalue its currency, hurting our exports and overwhelming us with imports." He wondered if his father's description of the 1930s, "a scary 10 years," would fit the 2000s.

He suspected the U.S. economic handlers—Treasury Secretary Rubin and Fed Chairman Greenspan—were putting a happy face on a grim situation. Though the Fed had proven it could quell inflation, he doubted it could foil deflation, the flip side of inflation (lower prices) and potentially just as dangerous. Already, deflation was spreading across Asia. Was the United States the next stop? "Deflation is tough to fight," Shelby said. "Lower interest rates won't do the trick, because banks aren't lending and companies aren't borrowing. Normally, companies borrow to expand, but now they're not expanding. In a deflationary crisis, they have no reason to expand because people aren't buying their products. People aren't buying because they're out of money."

Turning to the bright side, Shelby reminded himself that the Asian bear market offered U.S. multinationals a chance to go shopping with spare cash. When valuable assets went on the block in Japan, Korea, or Thailand, Citigroup and its ilk were there to snap them up. He thought the Japanese banking crisis wasn't as bad as the press made it out to be. "In some ways, the U.S. savings-and-loan crisis of the late 1980s was worse," he said. "Japan can borrow its way out of trouble with single-digit interest rates, while the U.S. government paid 9 percent on its S&L bailout bonds. Also, the Japanese consumer isn't saddled with bank and credit card debt the way U.S. consumers are."

Whatever happens, Shelby expected stocks to stop racing ahead and revert to their customary canter. "If the Dow continued to rise at the same pace it's risen over the past two decades, it would stand at roughly 100,000 two decades from now," he said. "But we're certain that won't happen. Even if the rise slows to 7 or 8 percent a year, the Dow could reach 40,000 to 50,000. So a lot more wealth can still be created long-term. On the other hand, the surge in corporate profits and P/E ratios that created the 1990s bonanza isn't likely to continue. It won't surprise me if the market is stuck in a trading range for the next five to ten years. Good stock pickers will make money, but the averages may not show much movement."

In the next comeuppance, whenever it occurs, Chris expects the growth-at-prudent-prices (GAPP) stocks will suffer less than growth-at-silly-prices (GASP) stocks. "One scenario has Mr. Market shedding 30 percent and the New York Venture Fund shedding 15," he said. "But there's no guarantee of that, and, anyway, if our Fund is down with the rest, nobody will congratulate the managers on losing less than the dart board. If a modern Cassandra tipped me off to the exact arrival date of the next bear, I'd raise cash to invest after the onslaught. But without a Cassandra, there's no way of timing calamity. If I prepare for the worst and stocks rise another 15 percent, I don't want my Fund to rise zero.

"Our best bear protection is buying companies with strong balance sheets, low debt, real earnings, and powerful franchises. These companies can survive bad times and eventually become more dominant as weaker competitors are forced to cut back or shut down."

In the early phase of the Chris–Ken collaboration, the New York Venture Fund has had its occasional midyear slump, but the comanagers ended the millennium on an upbeat note. According to Morningstar, New York Venture's recorded its sixth consecutive year of superior performance in its category, and Davis Financial had led its category for five straight years. The New York Venture Fund gained 10 percent in 2000 while the average stock lost that amount and the Nasdaq was having its 50-percent-off sale.

Chris sees making good investments as only part of the New York Venture Fund's job. Just as important is persuading clients to park their cash in the fund long enough to reap the benefit. As reported in *Mutual Funds* magazine (March 2000), typical investors stay with a typical fund less than three years. Then they're lured away by more exciting funds, just at the point when these others falter. This frequent switching has been costly. The average fund gained more than 500 percent between 1984 and 1998; the average owner gained only 186 percent. The rest was lost to the dating game. Lackluster funds were routinely dropped and replaced by more exciting funds, just at the point where the exciting funds lost their luster and the duller, spurned funds regained theirs.

In bad times, Chris hopes his customers will stick around for the inevitable rebound. "Our firm is devoted to educating customers to stay the course. We try not to be too positive about short-term successes, or too negative about short-term setbacks."

CHAPTER 11

INVESTING À LA DAVIS

IN THE FAST-GROWTH LANE, A FEW RELIABLE winners (the Microsofts and Wal-Marts) race ahead of the wanna-bes in every decade. Invest four figures in the next reliable winner and, 20 years later, you can retire with a seven-figure portfolio. Take Microsoft—and what investors don't wish they had? The stock looked extravagant at almost any time. It has continued to sell at a pricey 30 to 40 times earnings throughout its lucrative history. Yet, with the earnings doubling every 24 months, Microsoft buyers always found themselves holding a bargain two years after their "undisciplined" purchase. Their patience was well rewarded. A modest investment during Microsoft's infancy was as good as winning the lottery. What's the catch? Finding another Microsoft among the hopeful enterprises that annually go public in growing numbers. Picking the survivors, let alone the winners, is as hard as figuring out which turtle eggs hatched in the sand will become the giant turtles of the future. It's curious how few great fortunes have been made by fast-growth technology enthusiasts. Founders and other insiders have become wealthy on high-tech, but where are the outsiders' yachts? No high-tech stockpicker has

144

made the *Forbes* 400 list, perhaps because successful trendy investing demands contradictory abilities: the ability to see the next New New Thing and the courage to take a chance on it, plus the skepticism and the flexibility needed to abandon the New New Thing before it succumbs to the New New New Thing. People who stick too long with a technology play find their paper profits quickly vaporize, as they did in 1970 and can be expected to do in the future. Every trendy industry in one decade has a habit of destroying its backers in the next.

On the flip side of fast-growth investing is *value*. Value investors ignore the wanna-bes and concentrate on the has-beens. According to Benjamin Graham, the father of value investing, a perfect value play occurs when a company's tangible assets (cash in the bank, buildings, machines, and so on) will fetch more in a going-out-of-business sale than can be realized in the current market. This affords investors some margin of safety. If all goes badly, the company can be liquidated and they will get back more than they paid for their shares. The catch is: Value companies tend to have problems, and a stock that looks cheap today continues to get cheaper.

Between the fast growers that flame out and the value companies that limp along, there's a middle ground where companies offer steady profit growth at a value price. Generally, value prices don't exist in hot industries, so middle-ground investing automatically keeps adherents away from fanciful and dangerous territory like the Internet.

The Davises occupy this middle ground. They started with insurance stocks, and then, after a period of unfortunate fast-growth experimentation, Shelby applied his father's method to other industries, especially finance.

The math is instructive because the middle ground requires a longer wait for a big payday. Davis stayed with the middle ground for more than 40 years, but 40 years is exactly what a 30-year-old investor is looking at when he or she begins to prepare for retirement. "Investing isn't as complex as some people make it out to be," Chris volunteered. "You're deploying cash today, hoping to get more cash back in the future. That's all investing is. For us, the whole process hinges on two questions: What kind of businesses to buy, and how much to pay for them? To answer question one: A company worth buying makes more money than it spends. Its profit is recycled for maximum shareholder benefit. The second question, the price tag, is often ignored."

In the distant past, people bought stocks for their dividends, but dividends have gone the way of the manual toothbrush. Today, profit is paramount, and before Chris can determine whether the price tag is excessive, irresistible, or reasonable, he turns a skeptic's eye toward the earnings.

"We ask ourselves," said Chris, "if we owned the company outright, how much reward [would] we pocket at the end of the year, after reinvesting enough cash to maintain the status quo, and before reinvesting for growth? The result is called 'owner earnings.' This isn't a snap to calculate. We adjust for stock options, the depreciation rate, deferred taxes, and other subtle factors. Owner earnings are almost always lower than the earnings reported by the company.

"We also take a hard look at debt. Two businesses may have identical earnings and sell for the same price, so apparently they're valued the same. However, if one is saddled with a large debt and the other is debt-free, they're not the same at all."

Once Chris translates the often fanciful "reported" earnings into "owner earnings," he compares the expected future payoff from holding the stock to the payoff from holding a government bond. Bondholders receive predictable payments; a stock's benefits are potentially superior but often less reliable. [For purposes of comparison, Chris translates owner earnings into an "earnings yield" by dividing the earnings by the stock price—the inverse of the P/E ratio. Thus, a $30 stock that earns $2 (a P/E of 15) "yields" 6.6 percent, or more than a contemporary bond. But when a $60 stock earns $2 (a P/E of 30), it yields 3.3 percent, much less than a bond.]

"You'd be crazy to own a business that yields 3.3 percent instead of a 6 percent bond, unless the business can increase its earnings yield in the future," Chris says. "In other words, it must be able to grow."

"The challenge is to project that growth out eight or ten years. For any projection to be close to the mark, the business must be relatively predictable. You can't pin a ten-year forecast on the typical tech company. Even if you buy tech at a relatively cheap price (we picked up Hewlett-Packard at 15 times earnings), it can take years before the return on the stock matches the return on a bond." The Davis strategy—the result of five decades of trial, error, and refinement—worked its way through father, son, and grandsons, and each generation tweaked it and tuned it to fit the era. The 10 basic tenets remain the same:

1. *Avoid cheap stocks.* Shelby learned from experience, in the 1980s, that most cheap stocks deserve to be cheap because they're attached to poor companies. Chances are, a poor company will stay that way. Its CEO will predict better times ahead, as CEOs always do. The company may put itself in rehab, but rehab is an iffy proposition. "Even when it works," says Shelby, "it usually takes a company longer to turn around than anybody expects. You have to be a masochist to like this kind of investing."

2. *Avoid expensive stocks.* Stocks may deserve to be expensive because they're attached to great companies, but Shelby refuses to buy them unless they carry a sensible price tag, relative to their earnings. "No business is attractive at any price," says Shelby. The Davises never overpaid for clothes, houses, or vacations. Why should investors overpay for earnings, which after all, are what they're buying whenever they invest in a company?

Chris describes the fictional epitome of what's wrong with hot issues that fizzle: "Microscape Casino and Steakhouse." The stock symbol for this imaginary enterprise is GOGO. Is this an Internet café with slot machines? Who cares! Whatever it does, GOGO has a boffo debut. Buyers pay 30 times earnings for the shares, and, over a four-year stretch, GOGO grows its earnings at a gratifying 30 percent annual clip. In the fifth year, GOGO loses some pep; earnings are up "only" 15 percent. For most companies, 15 percent is a fine result, but GOGO investors expect more. Now, they're balking at the shares and paying half the prior multiple—15 times earnings. This results in a 50 percent "correction" in the price.

At this point, the paper profits vaporize, and any early buyer who held GOGO through its brief heyday is left with a paltry 6 percent annual return—hardly a fair compensation for the risk. U.S. government bonds paid 6 percent, and those were much less risky.

Once a fast grower disappoints, investors fall prey to cruel mathematics: a stock that's down 50 percent must rise 100 percent before it returns to the break-even point.

3. *Buy moderately priced stocks in companies that grow moderately fast.* Shelby's idea of a superior investment was a company that had a growth rate faster than the "multiple." He avoided GOGO and looked for companies like SOSO, an imaginary regional bank. SOSO, an unspectacular 13 percent earner, was selling for a modest 10 times its earnings. If SOSO continued to perform as advertised for five years, causing investors to pay 15 times earnings for the stock, the patient shareholder bagged a 20 percent annual return, as opposed to the 6 percent that would have been received from GOGO.

Occasionally, the Davis clan discovered a "stealth grower" with a SOSO reputation and Microsoft's knack for profit. Spectacular returns for a bleacher price is an irresistible combination, and Davis found it in AIG and numerous others.

Had AIG sold pacemakers or genetically altered seeds, investors surely would have awarded it a higher multiple. As a boring insurance company, it never attracted much exuberance—irrational or otherwise. That the stock was chronically undervalued kept the downside risk to a minimum.

4. *Wait until the price is right.* When Shelby liked a company but not the price tag, he waited for a chance to pay less. Analysts who changed their opinions three or four times a year created chances to buy IBM, Intel, and Hewlett-Packard. The occasional bear market also became the careful shopper's best friend. As Davis used to say, "Bear markets make people a lot of money, they just don't know it at the time."

Sometimes, an industry has its own bear market. The real estate bear of the 1980s spread into banking and gave Shelby a chance to buy Citicorp and Wells Fargo. The Clinton Administration's misguided health care reform package, in the early 1990s, sicced the bears on drug stocks, and first-rate pharmaceutical manufacturers (Merck, Pfizer, Lilly, etc.) were marked down 40 to 50 percent. Shelby and Chris built positions in all three.

An individual company can have its own bear market when bad news (an oil spill, a class action lawsuit, a product recall, and so on) sinks the stock. This is a buying opportunity, as long as the calamity is short-lived and doesn't hinder the company's long-term prospects.

"When you buy a battered stock in a solid company," Shelby says, "you take some risk out of the purchase. Investors have low expectations."

Through the 1980s, Shelby could choose from an ample selection of growth companies selling at 10 to 12 times earnings. These all but disappeared in the Roaring '90s. More than ever before, Chris and Ken were forced to wait for a markdown.

5. *Don't fight progress.* Shelby chose his tech stocks carefully, but he didn't avoid them entirely, as two well-known technophobes, Buffett and Peter Lynch, had done.

As long as he could find companies at value prices with real earnings and established franchises, he was eager to invite technology into his portfolio. Otherwise, he'd miss the liveliest part of the economy. He bought Intel early and rode it to a fantastic gain. He owned IBM since the mid-1980s. He bought Applied Materials, a modern "pick-and-shovel play." In the Gold Rush of the nineteenth century, merchants who sold picks and shovels made ample profit, but their prospecting customers went broke. In similar fashion, Applied Materials sold equipment to prospectors in the semiconductor industry.

6. *Invest in a theme.* "Bottoms-up" stockpickers invest in companies that have favorable attributes. They'll buy an oil driller as readily as a fast-food chain, if the story is promising. A "top-down" stockpicker surveys the economic climate, finds industries that are likely to thrive in current conditions, and chooses companies from those industries. Shelby is "top down" and "bottoms up." Before he puts new cash to work, he looks for "themes." Most of the time, themes are obvious.

In the 1970s, the obvious theme was rampant inflation. Shelby filled the New York Venture Fund with oil, natural gas, aluminum, and other commodity-based companies that stood to profit from higher prices. In the 1980s, there were signs the Fed was winning its war against inflation. Shelby found a new theme: lower prices and lower interest rates. He cut back on the hard assets and bought financial assets: banks, brokerage houses, and insurance companies. A financial group benefits from falling interest rates. Shelby sank 40 percent of his fund's assets into financials, just in time for their great leap forward. These "stealth growth stocks" didn't increase profits as fast as Microsoft or Home Depot, but they delivered happy returns nonetheless.

In the 1990s, Shelby and Chris acted on another obvious theme: aging baby boomers. As the wealthiest generation in U.S. history approached geezerdom, drug companies, health care, and nursing homes were beneficiaries. After a big run-up in drug stocks, Shelby waited to buy at the next markdown.

7. *Let your winners ride.* The typical growth-stock mutual fund sells 90 percent of its holdings every year and replaces them with other, presumably more promising merchandise. The turnover rate at New York Venture Fund hovers around 15 percent. The Davises prefer to buy and hold, primarily because they avoid paying the huge capital gains taxes on their long-term gains. The buy-and-hold approach keeps transaction costs low and eliminates mistakes that happen with frequent trading. Frequent traders are just as likely to trade a winner for a loser and vice versa.

Throughout Shelby's childhood, Davis harped on the futility of market timing. Shelby passed the message along to Chris and Andrew.

"We buy at a bargain price we can live with for a long time," Shelby says. "Eventually, we hope to see the stock sell at 'fair value,' and once it reaches that point, we tend to keep it as long as earnings continue to rise. We like to buy at a value price but we want to end up with growth companies.

"I was comfortable owning a stock through two or three recessions, or market cycles. That way, I learned how the company handled bad times, as well as good times."

8. *Bet on superior management.* Davis invested in great managers like Hank Greenberg at AIG. Shelby did the same with Andy Grove at Intel and Eli Broad at SunAmerica. If a great leader left one company for another, Shelby moved money into the new enterprise, buying the manager's talent again. When Jack Grundhoffer switched from Wells Fargo to First Bank Systems, Shelby bought First Bank. He bought American Express when Harvey Golub surfaced there.

"It's a Wall Street truism that good management is important to any company's success, but the typical analyst's report ignores the subject," says Chris. "Analysts prefer to discuss the latest numbers, but we never buy anything without assessing the leadership."

9. *Ignore the rear-view mirror.* "Computers and their endless databases cause investors to focus on the past," says Shelby. "More than ever before, people are looking backward into the future." The most valuable lesson to learn from history on Wall Street is that history doesn't exactly repeat itself. For 25 years after the 1929 Crash, hordes of investors avoided stocks on the false premise that a 1929 rerun was imminent. After World War II, they avoided stocks because they'd learned wars are always followed by recessions. In the second half of the 1970s, they avoided stocks and prepared for a repeat of the 1973 to 1974 bear market. As Shelby wrote in 1979, "The majority of investors today are spending an inordinate amount of time defensing against what we believe is an improbable if not almost impossible decline of similar magnitude." From 1988 to 1989, they avoided stocks and prepared for a repeat of the 1987 Crash. In all cases, they wished they hadn't. Numerous fallacious lessons have been learned from Wall Street experience. For example:

- "Stocks only rise when corporate profits rise." Actually, stocks often do well when profits sag.
- "Stocks are hurt by high inflation." They weren't hurt during the early 1950s.
- "Stocks are a perfect hedge against high inflation." Not in the early 1970s.

10. *Stay the course.* "Stocks may be risky for one, three, or even five years, but not 10 or 15 years," says Chris. "My father got in at a market top and, 20 years later, his bad start was irrelevant. In our messages to shareholders, we keep repeating ourselves: We're running in a marathon."

In the months this book went through the editing gauntlet, owners of tech stocks or tech mutual funds saw for themselves

The Davis Checklist

As Shelby and Chris noted in a memo written on May 22, 1997, every company they installed in the New York Venture Fund's portfolio exhibited most, if not all, of the following characteristics:

- First-class management with a proven record of keeping its word.
- Does innovative research and uses technology to maximum advantage.
- Operates abroad as well as at home. Overseas markets have given mature U.S. companies a second chance at fast growth. Some Wall Street analysts dubbed Coca-Cola a has-been in the early 1980s, but Coke went abroad and proved them wrong. The story was the same for AIG, McDonald's, and Philip Morris.
- Sells products or services that don't become obsolete.
- Insiders own a large chunk of shares and have a personal stake in the company's success.
- Company deliver strong returns on investors' capital, and managers are committed to rewarding investors.
- Expenses are kept to a minimum, which makes the company a low-cost producer.
- Company enjoys a dominant or a growing share in a growing market.
- Company is adept at acquiring competitors and making them more profitable.
- Company has a strong balance sheet.

the perils of growth at any price, in the collapse of the Nasdaq market. Cheerleaders of the new-era concept gained a retroactive respect for old-era concepts—crusty truisms about overheated markets always finding a way to cool down. Whether we've found the bottom of this latest bear market, or whether the bottom is yet to be reached is anybody's guess, but already the decline of 2000/2001 has cost investors trillions and demoralized the stock-hungry public. It also has brought the market closer to the Davis comfort zone, where money can be made buying companies at less than 15 times earnings and investing in the 7 to 15 percent annual earnings growth that has been the norm for many decades.

Through difficult times, the Davis family has found solace in the Rule of 72, realizing that if you can manage to compound your money at 10 percent per year, you'll be well rewarded, and if you can compound at 15 percent or better (as Davis did with his own portfolio and as Shelby did with the New York Venture Fund), you'll enjoy an enormous return that will make the recent setback seem as a trivial feint. Patience, long-term thinking, and a generational time frame make up the Davises's recipe for successful investing.

Figure 11.1 Davis New York Venture Fund Class A Shares (February 17, 1969, to December 31, 2000). Fund performance includes 4.75 percent maximum sales share and reflects reinvested distributions and changes in net asset value for Class A shares.

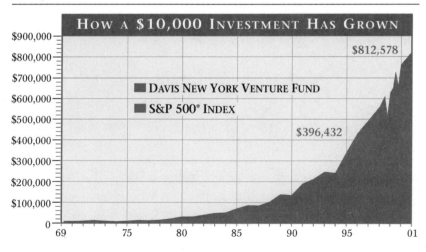

154